The Future of
Islam

The Future of
Islam

WILFRED S. BLUNT

NONSUCH

"La taknatu addurru yontharu akduhu
Liauda ahsana fin nithami wa ajmala."

"Fear not. Often pearls are unstrung
To be put in better order."

First published 1882
Copyright © in this edition 2007
Nonsuch Publishing Ltd

Nonsuch Publishing (Ireland)
73 Lower Leeson Street, Dublin 2

Nonsuch Publishing (UK)
Cirencester Road, Chalford, Stroud, Gloucestershire, GL6 8PE

www.nonsuch-publishing.com

Nonsuch Publishing Ltd is an imprint of NPI Media Group

British Library Cataloguing in Publication Data.
A catalogue record for this book is available from the British Library.

ISBN 978 1 84588 569 4

Typesetting and origination by Nonsuch Publishing Limited
Printed in Great Britain by Oaklands Book Services Limited

Contents

Preface

These essays, written for the *Fortnightly Review* in the summer and autumn of 1881, were intended as first sketches only of a maturer work which the author hoped, before giving finally to the public, to complete at leisure, and develop in a form worthy of critical acceptance, and of the great subject he had chosen. Events, however, have marched faster than he at all anticipated, and it has become a matter of importance with him that the idea they were designed to illustrate should be given immediate and full publicity. The French, by their invasion of Tunis, have precipitated the Mohammedan movement in North Africa; Egypt has roused herself for a great effort of national and religious reform; and on all sides Islam is seen to be convulsed by political portents of ever-growing intensity. He believes that his countrymen will in a very few months have to make their final choice in India, whether they will lead or be led by the wave of religious energy which is sweeping eastwards, and he conceives it of consequence that at least they should know the main issues of the problem before them. To shut their eyes to the great facts of contemporary history, because that history has no immediate connection with their daily life, is a course unworthy of a great nation; and in England, where the opinion of the people guides the conduct of affairs, can hardly fail to bring disaster. It should be remembered that the modern British Empire, an agglomeration of races ruled by public opinion in a remote island, is an experiment new in the history of the world, and needs justification in exceptional enlightenment; and it must be remembered, too, that no empire ever yet was governed without a living policy. The author, therefore, has resolved to publish his work, crude as it is, without more delay, in the hope that it may be instrumental in guiding the national choice. He is, nevertheless, fully aware of its defects both in accuracy and completeness, and he can only hope that they may be pardoned him in view of the general truth of the picture he has drawn.

Since the last of these essays was written, their author has returned to Egypt, and has there had the satisfaction of finding the ideas, vaguely foreshadowed by him as the dream of some few liberal Ulema of the Azhar, already a practical reality. Cairo has now declared itself as the home of progressive thought in Islam, and its university as the once more independent seat of Arabian theology. Secured from Turkish interference by the national movement of the Arabs, the Ulema of the Azhar have joined heart and soul with the party of reform. The importance of this event can hardly be overrated; and if, as now seems probable, a liberal Mohammedan Government by a free Mohammedan people should establish itself firmly on the Nile, it is beyond question that the basis of a social and political Reformation for all Islam has been laid. It is more than all a hopeful sign that extreme moderation with regard to the Caliphate is observed by the Egyptian leaders. Independence, not opposition, is the motto of the party; and no rent has been made or is contemplated by them in the orthodox coat of Islam. Abd el Hamid Khan is still recognized as the actual Emir el Mumenin, and the restoration of a more legitimate Caliphate is deferred for the day when its fate shall have overtaken the Ottoman Empire. This is as it should be. Schism would only weaken the cause of religion, already threatened by a thousand enemies; and the premature appearance of an Anti-Caliph in Egypt or Arabia, however legitimate a candidate he might be by birth for the office, would divide the Mohammedan world into two hostile camps, and so bring scandal and injury on the general cause. In the meantime, however, liberal thought will have a fair field for its development, and can hardly fail to extend its influence wherever the Arabic language is spoken, and among all those races which look on the Azhar as the centre of their intellectual life. This is a notable achievement, and one which patience may turn, perhaps in a very few years, to a more general triumph. There can be little doubt now that the death of Abd el Hamid, or his fall from Empire, will be the signal for the return of the Caliphate to Cairo, and a formal renewal there by the Arabian mind of its lost religious leadership.

To Mohammedans the author owes more than a word of apology. A stranger and a sojourner among them, he has ventured on an exposition of their domestic griefs, and has occasionally touched the ark of their religion with what will seem to them a profane hand; but his motive has been throughout a pure one, and he trusts that they will pardon him in virtue of the sympathy with them which must be apparent in every line that he has written. He has predicted for them great political misfortunes in the immediate future, because he believes that these are a necessary step in the process of their spiritual development; but he has a supreme confidence in Islam, not only as a spiritual, but as a temporal system the heritage and gift of the Arabian race, and capable of satisfying their most civilized wants; and he believes in the hour of their political resurgence. In the meantime he is convinced that he serves their interests best by speaking what he holds to be the truth regarding their situation. Their day of empire has all but passed away, but there remains to them a day of social independence better than empire. Enlightened, reformed and united in sympathy, Mussulmans need not fear political destruction in their original homes, Arabia, Egypt, and North Africa; and these must suffice them as a Dar el Islam till better days shall come. If the author can do anything to help them to preserve that independence they may count upon him freely within the limits of his strength, and he trusts to prove to them yet his sincerity in some worthier way than by the publication of these first essays.

CAIRO,
January 15th, 1882

Introduction to the Modern Edition

Wilfred Scawen Blunt was, in many respects, an unlikely champion of the Islamic world. Abandoning the confines of a diplomatic career to devote himself to a life of adventure and personal intrigue, this 'brilliant eccentric' went on to scandalize Victorian Britain with his numerous love affairs and unconventional views on politics and religion. A poet who married Byron's granddaughter and entertained the likes of Oscar Wilde and W.B. Yeats at his literary salons, Blunt was also a political iconoclast who dared question Britain's ambitions during its colonial heyday; a frequently contrary rebel always in search of a cause, whether it was Egyptian nationalism, Irish Home Rule or India's struggles. To Lord Curzon, he was an 'incorrigible charlatan'; to his estranged daughter, a narcissistic and wily cad. "Exultantly vain, he flung his challenge to the world," she complained, "a pirate of the sea, a follower of Casanova and *Les Liaisons Dangereuses*."

But the man who penned the series of essays which would eventually be published as *The Future of Islam* was also a distinguished Arabist and astute observer of currents lapping at the wider shores of the Islamic world in the twilight decades of the Ottoman empire. Like T.E. Lawrence, who would later hail him a "prophet and role-model", Blunt loved the romance of the desert and some of his first trips to the Middle East involved exploring remote tribal regions bordering the Euphrates and the Najd. While these journeys were undertaken as part of his wife's mission to export thoroughbred Arabian horses to England, they also allowed Blunt to see Islam as it was lived by ordinary Bedouins, an experience that would foster his vision of a 'pure' faith untainted by the excesses of the Ottoman empire.

Having abandoned his own Catholic faith after reading Darwin, Blunt admired and respected Islam to the point of considering conversion. "He began to wonder whether a reformed Islam did not hold the solution he had looked for but failed to find in Catholicism", noted his biographer, Elizabeth Longford. "A dogmatic creed to satisfy his heart, but one so simple as not to affront his intellect." The more Blunt travelled in the Islamic world, from Jeddah to Cairo and Istanbul, the more convinced he became that if Arab Muslims were to shrug off the tyrannical, decadent rule of the Turks, then and only then would Islam be able to undergo a true spiritual revival. For Blunt, reformed Islam meant a creed cleansed of Ottoman influence and firmly anchored in its Arab roots. "If I can introduce a pure Arabian breed of horses into England and help to see Arabia free of the Turks, I shall not have quite lived in vain," he wrote in 1880.

It was in Egypt that Blunt came across a small band of reformers leading the nascent modernist movement in Islam, individuals such as Jamal-al-Din Al Afghani and his disciple Mohammad Abduh. Both advocated religious reform capable of meeting the challenges of modernity, envisaging the birth of a pan-Islamic consciousness that would act as a bulwark against Europe's colonialist surge. Both would prove pivotal to the development of Blunt's ideas on the Islamic world and its relations with the West. "If the Islamic nation is to emerge from its state of dependency and subjugation to foreign powers, there is but one successful remedy," Afghani, whom Blunt called a 'wild man of genius,' wrote: "to return to the bases of religion, comply with its original strictures, seek guidance from its abundant spiritual counsel toward purity of heart and moral refinement ... The true fundaments of religion, unadulterated by subsequent innovations, give nations the power of unity, inspire them to acquire virtue and expand the scope of knowledge, and lead them to highest ends of modernity."

Many proponents of this Islamic liberation theology, including Blunt, believed the concept of caliphate should be reclaimed from the dying Ottoman empire by establishing an Arab caliphate, the spiritual authority of which would be recognized universally. Blunt sided with those who argued that classical traditions of caliphate demanded the caliph be descended from the Prophet Muhammad's tribe, and therefore Arab.

These ideas came together to form the basis for Blunt's writings on Islam, essays that, when they first appeared in a British journal in 1881, proved as pioneering as the proposals they set forth. Blunt was not the first eminent Victorian to wander across vast swathes of the Islamic world in order to divine its mysteries—Richard Burton, after all, had written about entering Mecca and Medina in disguise some thirty years before—but his examination of the state of the Islamic world was quite unique for its time. Writing of the work in later years, he said: "In it I committed myself without reserve to the Cause of Islam as essentially the 'Cause of Good' over an immense portion of the world, and to be encouraged, not repressed, by all who cared for the welfare of mankind."

Devoid of sensationalism, his was a sympathetic yet measured treatment of Islam as it stood some twelve centuries after its birth. Blunt explained the tenets, structure and origins of Islam, along with its evolution and political history in a simple, coherent way—a novel approach at a time when most writing on Muslims tended to be accompanied by predictable references to fanaticism. He emphasized the political and cultural diversity of the Islamic world, drawing attention to the millions of Muslims in South and South East Asia as well as offering a perceptive analysis of why the creed appealed so much to its "vast and yet uncounted" adherents in sub-Saharan Africa.

It was, Blunt wrote, a "bird's-eye view" of Islam addressed to "practical Englishmen" in the hope "it may be instrumental in guiding the national choice"—that is, British foreign policy. Blunt's treatise was very much to do with how Britain could better position herself in the face of a crumbling Ottoman empire. In-depth knowledge of the Islamic world was paramount, as without it "it would be almost impossible to make clear the problem presented to us by modern Islam or guess its solutions."

Blunt's reputation among Muslims in the Middle East and Asia flourished, firing his sense of mission and appealing to his self-importance. He declared: "The Muslims have no better friend than I." If he were lying on his deathbed, he mused, "I would have made my profession of Islam and attained perhaps to the honour of Mohammedan saintship, so great was the devotion of all the community to me." Blunt was beginning to imagine himself "the rising prophet of the new [phase] ... which would see a regeneration of Islam with England's help in Arabia." The task fell to Britain alone, he claimed, because it had an historical tolerance towards Islam greater than what he refers to as "the Crusading States" of continental Europe. While Islam's reformation could only come from within, Britain had a crucial role to play as the world's greatest power. It would, he hoped, "take Islam by the hand and encourage her boldly in the path of virtue. This is the only worthy course, and the only wise one—wiser and worthier, I venture, than a whole century of crusade."

Keeping in mind those "practical Englishmen" of the Establishment he imagined his readers to be, Blunt outlined the rewards such a policy could bring for his country. He may have been a fervent anti-colonialist, but Blunt was not immune to pandering to Britain's imperialist conceits. An Arab caliphate based in the holy city of Mecca would ideally exist under British protection, he proposed, and given Britain's dominion in India, home to the world's largest and wealthiest Muslim population, Queen Victoria could then make herself "in some sort the political head of Islam … and be left its most powerful sovereign … [with] the power and the opportunity to a degree never yet presented to any Christian government of directing the tone of thought of Mussulmans throughout the world."

In addition to providing a way of expanding and consolidating influence within its existing Muslim territories and warding off hostility from others, he wrote, Britain could also benefit from having a stake in revenues culled from pilgrims to Mecca and Medina.

Events in Egypt and North Africa prompted him to introduce a note of caution by the time the essays were published in book form in 1882. In the introduction to *The Future of Islam* he wrote that "the restoration of a more legitimate [i.e., Arab] Caliphate is deferred for the day when its fate shall have overtaken the Ottoman Empire. This is as it should be. Schism would only weaken the cause of religion, already threatened by a thousand enemies; and the premature appearance of an Anti-Caliph in Egypt or Arabia … would divide the Mohammedan world into two hostile camps, and so bring scandal and injury on the general cause."

The Foreign Office mandarins to whom Blunt presented his proposal were not impressed, however, and his dreams of Islamic regeneration led by an Arab caliph and guided by Britain foundered.

Some decades later an admiring T.E. Lawrence would take up a diluted version of Blunt's plan to encourage the Arab Revolt against Ottoman rule. Blunt's vision of an Arabian caliphate never materialized, however, and in 1924 the fledgling Turkish republic abolished the institution as part of Ataturk's sweeping reforms.

Blunt continued his quest for Islamic renewal right up to the turn of the century, travelling to Egypt, India and even the Ottoman sultan's palace in his fruitless search for a suitable actor and stage to lead a reformation of the faith. Growing increasingly disillusioned, in 1887 he declared "the East has become an irritant". Ten years later he returned to the desert, this time northwestern Egypt, to rediscover the "pure" Islam that had so impressed him years before. An altercation with armed villagers left him bitter, triggering a sense that his hopes for Islamic reform had been fanciful and naive. "I had made myself a romance about these reformers", he wrote afterwards, "but it has no substantial basis ... The less religion in the world perhaps, after all, the better."

Blunt's legacy has been interpreted in many different ways. Edward Said wrote that of all the nineteenth-century Orientalists, Blunt was by far the most sympathetic. Some writers have commended what they see as his sincere commitment to the cause of progress in the Muslim world. But the extent of that commitment has also been questioned, with some pointing out the irony that despite being a staunch opponent of imperialism, many of Blunt's ideas were ultimately used to serve its ends. Others go further, portraying him as supporting pan-Islamism purely out of self-interest, cannily seeing its value as a tool to further partisan political strategies.

After decades of being little known outside academic circles, Blunt's writing on Islam has received more attention in the years since 9/11. While the goal of re-establishing the caliphate may now be the preserve of Osama bin Laden and radical groups such as Hizb ut-Tahrir, Blunt's emphasis on the common humanity shared by East and West is held up as a valuable message in an era dominated by theories claiming an inevitable "clash of civilizations" between Islam and the rest of the world. His insight into tensions between Islam's reactionary and reformist elements is as relevant today as it was in the late nineteenth century. Likewise his warnings against employing "social hostility and political aggression" in dealing with the Islamic world, or confronting Muslims under the name of "civilization" seem worthy of consideration some five years into a so-called "War on Terror" that has caused relations between Islam and the West to plummet.

More than anything, Blunt stressed the need for respect and recognition beyond simple stereotypes. While his dream of an Arab caliphate as some sort of Islamic papacy may now seem the stuff of a romantic idealist, it is his essential plea for mutual understanding that endures. "It is surely time that moral sympathy should unite the two great bodies of men who believe in and worship the same God", he wrote. "England, at least, may afford now to acknowledge Mohammedanism as something not to be merely combated and destroyed, but to be accepted by her and encouraged—accepted as a fact which for good or evil will exist in the world whether she will or no—encouraged because it has in it possibilities of good which she cannot replace by any creed or philosophy of her own. She can do much to help these possibilities ..."

Mary Fitzgerald
February, 2007

I

Census of the
Mohammedan World

The Haj

In the lull, which we hope is soon to break the storm of party strife in England, it may not perhaps be impossible to direct public attention to the rapid growth of questions which for the last few years have been agitating the religious mind of Asia, and which are certain before long to present themselves as a very serious perplexity to British statesmen; questions, moreover, which if not dealt with by them betimes, it will later be found out of their power to deal with at all, though a vigorous policy at the present moment might yet solve them to this country's very great advantage.

The revival which is taking place in the Mohammedan world is indeed worthy of every Englishman's attention, and it is difficult to believe that it has not received anxious consideration at the hands of those whose official responsibility lies chiefly in the direction of Asia; but I am not aware that it has hitherto been placed in its true light before the English public, or that a quite definite policy regarding it may be counted on as existing in the counsels of the present Cabinet. Indeed, as regards the Cabinet, the reverse may very well be the case. We know how suspicious English politicians are of policies which may be denounced by their enemies as speculative; and it is quite possible that the very magnitude of the problem to be solved in considering the future of Islam may have caused it to be put aside there as one "outside the sphere of practical politics." The phrase is a convenient one, and is much used by those in power amongst us who would evade the labour or the responsibility of great decisions. Yet that such a problem exists in a new and very serious form I do not hesitate to affirm, nor will my proposition, as I think, be doubted by any who have mingled much in the last few years with the Mussulman populations of Western Asia. There it is easily discernible that great changes are impending, changes perhaps analogous to those which Christendom underwent four hundred years ago, and that a new departure is urgently demanded of England if she would maintain even for a few years her position as the guide and arbiter of Asiatic progress.

It was not altogether without the design of gaining more accurate knowledge than I could find elsewhere on the subject of this Mohammedan revival that I visited Jeddah in the early part of the past winter, and that I subsequently spent some months in Egypt and Syria in the almost exclusive society of Mussulmans. Jeddah, I argued, the seaport of Mecca and only forty miles distant from that famous centre of the Moslem universe, would be the most convenient spot from which I could obtain such a bird's-eye view of Islam as I was in search of; and I imagined rightly that I should there find myself in an atmosphere less provincial than that of Cairo, or Bagdad, or Constantinople.

Jeddah is indeed in the pilgrim season the suburb of a great metropolis, and even a European stranger there feels that he is no longer in a world of little thoughts and local aspirations. On every side the politics he hears discussed are those of the great world, and the religion professed is that of a wider Islam than he has been accustomed to in Turkey or in India. There every race and language are represented, and every sect. Indians, Persians, Moors, are there,—negroes from the Niger, Malays from Java, Tartars from the Khanates, Arabs from the French Sahara, from Oman and Zanzibar, even, in Chinese dress and undistinguishable from other natives of the Celestial Empire, Mussulmans from the interior of China. As one meets these walking in the streets, one's view of Islam becomes suddenly enlarged, and one finds oneself exclaiming with Sir Thomas Browne, "Truly the (Mussulman) world is greater than that part of it geographers have described." The permanent population, too, of Jeddah is a microcosm of Islam. It is made up of individuals from every nation under heaven. Besides the indigenous Arab, who has given his language and his tone of thought to the rest, there is a mixed resident multitude descended from the countless pilgrims who have remained to live and die in the holy cities. These preserve, to a certain extent, their individuality, at least for a generation or two, and maintain a connection with the lands to which they owe their origin and the people who were their countrymen. Thus there is constantly found at Jeddah a free mart of intelligence for all that is happening in the world; and the common gossip of the bazaar retails news from every corner of the Mussulman earth. It is hardly too much to say that one can learn more of modern Islam in a week at Jeddah than in a year elsewhere, for there the very shopkeepers discourse of things divine, and even the Frank Vice-Consuls prophesy. The Hejazi is less shy, too, of discussing religious matters than his fellow Mussulmans are in other places. Religion is, as it were, part of his stock-in-trade, and he is accustomed to parade it before strangers. With a European he may do this a little disdainfully, but still he will do it, and with less disguise or desire to please than is in most places the case. Moreover—and this is important—it is almost always the practical side of questions that the commercial Jeddan will put forward. He sees things from a political and economical point of view, rather than a doctrinal, and if fanatical, he is so from the same motives, and no others, which once moved the citizens of Ephesus to defend the worship of their shrines.

In other cities, Cairo and Constantinople excepted, the Ulema, or learned men, of whom a stranger might seek instruction, would be found busying themselves mainly with doctrinal matters not always interesting at the present day, old-world arguments of Koranic interpretation which have from time immemorial occupied the schools. But here even these are treated practically, and as they bear on the political aspect of the hour. For myself, I became speedily impressed with the advantage thus afforded me, and neglected no opportunity which offered itself for listening and asking questions, so that without pretending to the possession of more special skill than any intelligent inquirer might command, I obtained a mass of information I cannot but think to be of great value—while this in its turn served me later as an introduction to such Mussulman divines as I afterwards met in the North. Jeddah then realized all my hopes and gratified nearly all my curiosities. I will own, too, to having come away with more than a gratified curiosity, and to having found new worlds of thought and life in an atmosphere I had fancied to be only of decay. I was astonished at the vigorous life of Islam, at its practical hopes and fears in this modern nineteenth century, and above all at its reality as a moral force; so that if I had not exactly come to scoff, I certainly remained, in a certain sense, to pray. At least I left it interested, as I had never thought to be, in the great struggle which seemed to me impending between the parties of reaction in Islam and reform, and not a little hopeful as to its favourable issue. What this is likely to be I now intend to discuss.

First, however, it will I think be as well to survey briefly the actual composition of the Mohammedan world. It is only by a knowledge of the elements of which Islam is made up that we can guess its future, and these are less generally known than they should be. A stranger from

Europe visiting the Hejaz is, as I have said, irresistibly struck with the vastness of the religious world in whose centre he stands. Mohammedanism to our Western eyes seems almost bounded by the limits of the Ottoman Empire. The Turk stands in our foreground, and has stood there from the days of Bajazet, and in our vulgar tongue his name is still synonymous with Moslem, so that we are apt to look upon him as, if not the only, at least the chief figure of Islam. But from Arabia we see things in a truer perspective, and become aware that beyond and without the Ottoman dominions there are races and nations, no less truly followers of the Prophet, beside whom the Turk shrinks into numerical insignificance. We catch sight, it may be for the first time in their real proportions, of the old Persian and Mogul monarchies, of the forty million Mussulmans of India, of the thirty million Malays, of the fifteen million Chinese, and the vast and yet uncounted Mohammedan populations of Central Africa. We see, too, how important is still the Arabian element, and how necessary it is to count with it, in any estimate we may form of Islam's possible future. Turkey, meanwhile, and Constantinople, retire to a rather remote horizon, and the Mussulman centre of gravity is as it were shifted from the north and west towards the south and east.

I was at some pains while at Jeddah to gain accurate statistics of the Haj according to the various races and sects composing it, and with them of the populations they in some measure represent. The pilgrimage is of course no certain guide as to the composition of the

Mussulman world, for many accidents of distance and political circumstance interfere with calculations based on it. Still to a certain extent a proportion is preserved between it and the populations which supply it; and in default of better, statistics of the Haj afford us an index not without value of the degree of religious vitality existing in the various Mussulman countries. My figures, which for convenience I have arranged in tabular form, are taken principally from an official record, kept for some years past at Jeddah, of the pilgrims landed at that port, and checked as far as European subjects are concerned by reference to the consular agents residing there. They may therefore be relied upon as fairly accurate; while for the land pilgrimage I trust in part my own observations, made three years ago, in part statistics obtained at Cairo and Damascus. For the table of population in the various lands of Islam I am obliged to go more directly to European sources of information. As may be supposed, no statistics on this point of any value were obtainable at Jeddah; but by taking the figures commonly given in our handbooks, and supplementing and correcting these by reference to such persons as I could find who knew the countries, I have, I hope, arrived at an approximation to the truth, near enough to give a tolerable idea to general readers of the numerical proportions of Islam. Strict accuracy, however, I do not here pretend to, nor would it if obtainable materially help my present argument.

The following is my table:—

Table of the Mecca Pilgrimage of 1880

Nationality of Pilgrims	Arriving by Sea	Arriving by Land	Total of Mussulman Population represented
Ottoman subjects including pilgrims from Syria and Irak, but not from Egypt or Arabia proper	8,500	1,000	22,000,0000
Egyptians	5,000	1,000	5,000,000
Mogrebbins ("people of the West"), that is to say Arabic-speaking Mussulmans from the Barbary States, Tripoli, Tunis, Algiers, and Morocco. These are always classed together and are not easily distinguishable from each other	6,000	n/a	18,000,000
Arabs from Yemen	3,000	n/a	2,500,000
Arabs from Oman and Hadramaut	3,000	n/a	3,000,000
Arabs from Nied, Assir, and Hasa, most of them Wahhabites	n/a	5,000	4,000,000
Arabs from Hejaz, of these perhaps 10,000 Meccans	n/a	22,000	2,000,000
Negroes from Soudan	2,000	n/a	10,000,000
Negroes from Zanzibar	1,000	n/a	1,500,000
Malabari from the Cape of Good Hope	150	n/a	n/a
Persians	6,000	2,500	8,000,000
Indians (British subjects)	15,000	n/a	40,000,000

Malays, chiefly from Java and Dutch subjects	12,000	n/a	30,000,000
Chinese	100	n/a	15,000,000
Mongols from the Khanates, included in the Ottoman Haj	n/a	n/a	6,000,000
Lazis, Corcassiams, Tartars, etc (Russian subjects) included in the Ottoman Haj	n/a	n/a	5,000,000
Independent Afghans and Beluchis, included in the Indian and Persian Hajs	n/a	n/a	3,000,000
Total of Pilgrims present at Arafat	93,250		
Total Census of Islam	175,000,000		

The figures thus roundly given require explanation in order to be of their full value as a bird's-eye view of Islam. I will take them as nearly as possible in the order in which they stand, grouping them, however, for further convenience sake under their various sectarian heads, for it must be remembered that Islam, which in its institution was intended to be one community, political and religious, is now divided not only into many nations, but into many sects. All, however, hold certain fundamental beliefs, and all perform the pilgrimage to Mecca, where they meet on common ground, and it is to this latter fact that the importance attached to the Haj is mainly owing.

The main beliefs common to all Mussulmans are—

1. A belief in one true God, the creator and ordainer of all things.

2. A belief in a future life of reward or punishment.

3. A belief in a divine revelation imparted first to Adam and renewed at intervals to Noah, to Abraham, to Moses, and to Jesus Christ, and last of all in its perfect form to Mohammed. This revelation is not only one of dogma, but of practice. It claims to have taught an universal rule of life for all mankind in politics and legislation as well as in doctrine and in morals. This is called Islam.

4. A belief in the Koran as the literal word of God, and of its inspired interpretation by the Prophet and his companions, preserved through tradition (Hadith).[1]

These summed up in the well-known "Kelemat" or act of faith, "There is no God but God, and Mohammed is the apostle of God," form a common doctrinal basis for every sect of Islam—and also common to all are the four religious acts, prayer, fasting, almsgiving and pilgrimage, ordained by the Koran itself. On other points, however, both of belief and practice, they differ widely; so widely that the sects must be considered as not only distinct from, but hostile to, each other. They are nevertheless, it must be admitted, less absolutely irreconcileable than are the corresponding sects of Christianity, for all allow the rest to be distinctly within the pale of Islam, and they pray on occasion in each other's mosques and kneel at the same shrines on pilgrimage. Neither do they condemn each other's errors as altogether damnable—except, I believe, in the case of the Wahhabites, who accuse other Moslems of polytheism and idolatry. The census of the four great sects may be thus roughly given—

1. The Sunites or Orthodox Mohammedans 145,000,000
2. The Shiites or Sect of Ali 15,000,000
3. The Abadites (Abadhiyeh) 7,000,000
4. The Wahhabites 8,000,000

The *Sunites*, or People of the Path, are of course by far the most important of these. They stand in that relation to the other sects in which the Catholic Church stands to the various Christian heresies, and claim alone to represent that continuous body of tradition political and religious, which is the sign of a living church. In addition to the dogmas already mentioned, they hold that, after the Prophet and his companions, other authorised channels of tradition exist of hardly less authority with these. The sayings of the four first Caliphs, as collected in the first century of the Mohammedan era, they hold to be inspired and unimpeachable, as are to a certain extent the theological treatises of the four great doctors of Islam, the Imams Abu Hanifeh, Malek, Esh Shafy, and Hanbal, and after them, though with less and less authority, the "fetwas," or decisions of distinguished Ulema, down to the present day. The collected body of teaching acquired from these sources is called the Sheriat (in Turkey the Sheriati Sherifeh) and is the canon law of Islam. Nor is it lawful that this should be gainsaid; while the Imams themselves may not inaptly be compared to the fathers of our Christian Church. It is a dogma, too, with the Sunites that they are not only an ecclesiastical but a political body, and that among them is the living representative of the temporal power of the Prophet, in the person of his Khalifeh or successor, though there is much division of opinion as to the precise line of succession in the past and the legitimate ownership of the title in the present. But this is too intricate and important a matter to be entered on at present.

The Sunites are then the body of authority and tradition, and being more numerous than the other three sects put together in a proportion of four and a half to one, have a good right to treat these as heretics. It must not, however, be supposed that even the Sunites profess absolutely homogeneous opinions. The path of Orthodox Islam is no macadamised road such as the Catholic Church of Christendom has become, but like one of its own Haj routes goes winding on, a labyrinth of separate tracks, some near, some far apart, some clean out of sight of the rest. All lead, it is true, in the same main direction, and here and there in difficult ground where there is a mountain range to cross or where some defile narrows they are brought together, but otherwise they follow their own ways as the idiosyncrasy of race and disposition may dictate. There is no common authority in the world acknowledged as superior to the rest, neither is there any office corresponding even remotely with the infallible Papacy.

The Mohammedan nations have for the most part each its separate school, composed of its own Ulema and presided over by its own Grand Mufti or Sheykh el Islam, and these are independent of all external influence. If they meet at all it is at Mecca, but even at Mecca there is no college of cardinals, no central authority; and though occasionally cases are referred thither or to Constantinople or Cairo, the fetwas given are not of absolute binding power over the faithful in other lands. Moreover, besides these national distinctions, there are three recognized schools of theology which divide between them the allegiance of the orthodox, and which, while not in theory opposed, do in fact represent as many distinct lines of religious thought. These it has been the fashion with European writers to describe as sects, but the name sect is certainly inaccurate, for the distinctions recognisable in their respective teachings are not more clearly marked than in those of our own Church parties, the high, the low, and the broad. Indeed a rather striking analogy may be traced between these three phases of English church teaching and the three so-called "orthodox sects" of Islam. The three Mohammedan schools are the Hanefite, the Malekite, and the Shafite, while a fourth, the Hanbalite, is usually added, but it numbers at the present day so few followers that we need not notice it.[2] A few words will describe each of these.

The *Hanefite* school of theology may be described as the school of the upper classes. It is the high and dry party of Church and State, if such expressions can be used about Islam. To it belongs the Osmanli race, I believe without exception, the ruling race of the north, and their kinsmen who founded Empires in Central and Southern Asia. The official classes, too, in most parts of the world are Hanefite, including the Viceregal courts of Egypt, Tripoli, and Tunis, and it would seem the courts of most of the Indian princes. It is probably rather as a consequence of this than as its reason that it is the most conservative of schools, conservative in the true sense of leaving things exactly as they are. The Turkish Ulema have always insisted strongly on the dogma that the *ijtahad*, that is to say the elaboration of new doctrine, is absolutely closed; that nothing can be added to or taken away from the already existing body of religious law, and that no new *mujtahed*, or doctor of Islam, can be expected who shall adapt that law to the life of the modern world. At the same time, while obstinate in matters of opinion, Hanefism has become extremely lax as to practice. Its moral teaching is held, and I believe justly, to be adapted only too closely to the taste of its chief supporters. It is accused by its enemies of having given the sanction of its toleration to the moral disorders common among the Turks, their use of fermented drinks, their immoderate concubinage and other worse vices. It is, in fact, the official school of Ottoman orthodoxy. It embraces most of those who at the present day support the revived spiritual pretensions of Constantinople.

The pilgrimage then described in our table as Ottoman is mostly made up of men of this theological school. It must not, however, be supposed that anything like the whole number either of the 8500 pilgrims, or of the 22,000,000 population they represent, is composed of Turks. The true Ottoman Turk is probably now among the rarest of visitors to Mecca, and it is doubtful whether the whole Turkish census in Europe and in Asia amounts to more than four millions. With regard to the pilgrimage there is good reason why this should be the case. In Turkey, all the able-bodied young men, who are the first material of the Haj, are taken from other duties for military service, and hardly any now make their tour of the Kaaba except in the Sultan's uniform. Rich merchants, the second material of the Haj in other lands, are almost unknown among the Turks; and the officials, the only well-to-do class in the empire, have neither leisure nor inclination to absent themselves from their worldly business of intrigue.

Besides, the official Turk is already too civilized to put up readily with the real hardships of the Haj. In spite of the alleviations effected by the steam navigation of the Red Sea, pilgrimage is still no small matter, and once landed at Jeddah, all things are much as they were a hundred years ago, while the Turk has changed. With his modern notion of dress and comfort he may indeed be excused for shrinking from the quaint nakedness of the pilgrim garb and the bare-headed march to Arafat under a tropical sun. Besides, there is the land journey still of three hundred miles to make before he can reach Medina, and what to some would be worse hardship, a wearisome waiting afterwards in the unhealthy ports of Hejaz. The

Turkish official, too, has learned to dispense with so many of the forms of his religion that he finds no difficulty in making himself excuses here. In fact, he seldom or never now performs the pilgrimage.

The mass of the Ottoman Haj is made up of Kurds, Syrians, Albanians, Circassians, Lazis, and Tartars from Russia and the Khanates, of everything rather than real Turks. Nor are those that come distinguished greatly for their piety or learning. The school of St. Sophia at Constantinople has lost its old reputation as a seat of religious knowledge; and its Ulema are known to be more occupied with the pursuit of Court patronage than with any other science. So much indeed is this the case that serious students often prefer a residence at Bokhara, or even in the heretical schools of Persia, as a more real road to learning. Turkey proper boasts at the present day few theologians of note, and still fewer independent thinkers.

The Egyptian Haj is far more flourishing. Speaking the language of Arabia, the citizen of Cairo is more at home in the holy places than any inhabitant of the northern towns can be. The customs of Hejaz are very nearly his own customs, and its climate not much more severe than his. Cairo, too, can boast a far more ancient political connection with Mecca than Constantinople can, for as early as the twelfth century the Sultans of Egypt were protectors of the holy places, while even since the Ottoman conquest, the Caliph's authority in Arabia has been almost uninterruptedly interpreted by his representative at Cairo. So lately as 1840 this was the position of things at Mecca, and it is only since the opening of the Suez Canal that direct administration from Constantinople has been seriously attempted. To the present day the Viceroy of Egypt shares with the Sultan the privilege of sending a mahmal, or camel litter, to Mecca every year with a covering for the Kaaba. Moreover the Azhar mosque of Cairo is the great university of Arabic-speaking races, and its Ulema have the highest reputation of any in Islam. Egyptian influence, therefore, must be reckoned as an important element in the forces which make up Mohammedan opinion. The late Khedive, it is true, did much to impair this by his infidelity and his coquetteries with Europe, and under his reign the Egyptian Haj fell to a low level; but Mohammed Towfik, who is a sincere, though liberal Mussulman, has already restored much of his country's prestige at Mecca, and it is not unlikely that in time to come Egypt, grown materially prosperous, may once more take a leading part in the politics of Islam.[3] But of this later.

All three schools of theology are taught in the Azhar mosque, and Egyptians are divided, according to their class, between them. The Viceroy and the ruling clique, men of Ottoman origin, are Hanefites, and so too are the descendants of the Circassian Beys, but the leading merchants of Cairo and the common people of that city are Shafites, while the fellahin of the Delta are almost entirely Malekite. Malekite, too, are the tribes west of the Nile, following the general rule of the population of Africa.[4]

The *Malekite* school of religious thought differs widely from the Hanefite. If the latter has been described as the high Church party of Islam, this must be described as the low. It is puritanical, fierce in its dogma, severe in its morals, and those who profess it are undoubtedly the most fervent, the most fanatical of believers. They represent more nearly than any other Mussulmans the ancient earnestness of the Prophet's companions, and the sword in their hand is ever the sword of God. Piety too, ostensible and sincere, is found everywhere among the Malekites. Abd el Kader, the soldier saint, is their type; and holy men by hereditary profession abound among them.

The Malekites believe with earnest faith in things supernatural, dreaming prophetic dreams, and seeing miracles performed as every-day occurrences. With the Arabs of Africa, unlike their kinsmen in Arabia itself, to pray and fast is still a severe duty, and no class of Mussulmans are more devout on pilgrimage. In Algiers and Morocco it is as common for a young man of fortune to build a mosque as it is for him to keep a large stud of horses. To do so poses him in the world, and a life of prayer is strictly a life of fashion. With regard to morals he is severe where the Koran is severe, indulgent where it indulges. Wine with him is an abomination, and asceticism with regard to meat and tobacco is often practised by him. On the whole he is respectable and respected; but the reforms he would impose on Islam are too purely reactive to be altogether acceptable to the mass of Mohammedans or suited to the urgent necessities of the age. It is conceivable, however, that should the revival of Islam take the form of a religious war, the races of Africa may be found taking the leading part in it. Tripoli, Tunis, Algiers, and Morocco contain hardy races of fighting men who may yet trouble Europe; and fifty years of rule have not yet assimilated the French Sahara.

It is difficult to gain accurate statistics as to the proportion of pilgrims sent to Mecca by these various States, but it would seem the Algerian pilgrimage is the smallest. This is due mainly to hindrances raised by the French Government, whose policy it is to isolate their province from the rest of the Mussulman world. An Algerian pilgrim is called upon to produce the sum of 1000 francs before he is permitted to embark for Jeddah, and he is subjected to various other needless formalities. Still the number sent is large and their fervour undoubted, though the upper classes, from a fear of losing credit with the French authorities, rather hold aloof.

The mainstay of the Mogrebbin Haj are the Moors. These have an immense name for zeal and religious courage at Mecca, and for the great scrupulosity with which they perform their religious duties. There is too among the Moors a far wider level of theological education than among most Mussulmans. I made acquaintance while at Jeddah with a young Arab from Shinghiat in Senegal who, Bedouin as he was, was an Alem, and one sufficiently well versed in the Sheriat to be referred to more than once in my presence on points of religious law and literature. I expressed my surprise at finding a Bedouin thus learned, for he was evidently an Arab of the Arabs, but he told me his was no exceptional position, and that most Bedouins in Southern Morocco could read the Koran. The Moors would have a still higher position in Islam than that already given them were it not that they are on one point at variance with the mass of Sunites. They do not acknowledge the modern Caliphate. Those therefore of the Sunites who have acknowledged the Ottoman claim are at issue with the Moors. On all other points, however, the Moors are Sunites of the Sunites.

From the Moor to the negro is but a step, though it is a step of race, perhaps of species. The political and religious connection of Morocco with the Soudan is a very close one, and, whatever may be the future of the Mediterranean provinces fronting the Spanish coast, it cannot be doubted that the Moorish form of Mohammedanism will be perpetuated in Central Africa. It is there, indeed, that Islam has the best certainty of expansion and the fairest field for a propagation of its creed. Statistics, if they could be obtained, would, I am convinced, show an immense Mohammedan progress within the last hundred years among the negro races, nor is this to be wondered at. Islam has so much to offer to the children of Ham that it cannot fail to win them—so much more than any form of Christianity or European progress can give.

The Christian missionary makes his way slowly in Africa. He has no true brotherhood to offer the negro except in another life. He makes no appeal to a present sense of dignity in the man he would convert. What Christian missionary takes a negress to wife or sits with the negro wholly as an equal at meat? Their relations remain at best those of teacher with taught, master with servant, grown man with child. The Mohammedan missionary from Morocco meanwhile stands on a different footing. He says to the negro, "Come up and sit beside me. Give me your daughter and take mine. All who pronounce the formula of Islam are equal in this world and in the next." In becoming a Mussulman even a slave acquires immediate dignity and the right to despise all men, whatever their colour, who are not as himself. This is a bribe in the hand of the preacher of the Koran, and one which has never appealed in vain to the enslaved races of the world.[5] Central Africa then may be counted on as the inheritance of Islam at no very distant day. It is already said to count ten millions of Moslems.

The *Shafite* school, the third of the four "orthodox sects", is the most flourishing of all in point of numbers, and it has characteristics which mark it out as the one best adapted to survive in the struggle which is impending between the schools of religious thought in Islam. The Shafites may be compared to our broad Church, though without its immediate tendency to infidelity. With the Shafites there is a disposition to widen rather than to narrow the area of theology. The Hanefites and Malekites proclaim loudly that inquiry has been closed and change is impossible, but the Shafites are inclined to seek a new mujtahed who shall reconcile Islam with the modern conditions of the world. They feel that there is something wrong in things as they are, for Islam is no longer politically prosperous, and they would see it united once more and reorganized even at the expense of some dogmatic concessions. I know that many even of the Shafites themselves will deny this, for no Mussulman will willingly acknowledge that he is an advocate of change; but it is unquestionable that among members of their school such ideas are more frequently found than with the others.

Among the Shafites, too, ideas of a moral reformation find a footing, and they speak more openly than the rest their suspicion that the house of Othman, with its fornications and its bestialities and contempt of justice, has been the ruin of Islam. Arabian custom is the basis of its ideas upon this head, for most Arabs out of Africa if anything are Shafites; and it is the school of the virtuous poor rather than of the licentious rich. It is more humane in its bearing towards Jews and Christians, finding a common ground with them in the worship of the one true God, the moral law propounded at various times to man, and the natural distinction between right and wrong. I may exaggerate this, perhaps, but something of it certainly exists, and it is a feeling that is growing.

Shafism has its stronghold at Cairo, where the Sheykh el Islam has always belonged to this rite, but it is also the prevailing school in Asia wherever Mohammedanism has been introduced through the instrumentality of Arabian missionaries. In India the mass of the Mussulman population is Shafite, especially in Hyderabad and the Bombay Presidency, where the Arab element is strongest, while Hanefism is the school of the great people who derive their origin from the Mogul conquests, and of many of the Ulema who are in the habit of making their religious education complete in the Hanefite schools of Bokhara. Wahhabism, too, in the present century has taken great hold of the poorer classes, and within the last few years a Turkish propaganda has been at work among them with some success. But of this again later.

The Indian Haj is the most numerous, and represents the largest population of all on our list, and it is besides the most wealthy. The Indian Mussulman has less to fear from the climate of Arabia than the native of more northern lands, and few who can afford it fail to perform this religious duty at least once in their lives. The English Government neither checks nor encourages the Haj, and indeed of late years has shown a rather culpable negligence as to the interests of British subjects on pilgrimage. Such at least is the opinion I heard constantly given at Jeddah, and several recent incidents seem to prove that a little closer attention to this matter would be advisable. That ugly story which was told in our newspapers more than a year ago of the abandonment of a pilgrim ship in the Red Sea by her British captain is, I am sorry to say, a true one, and I heard it confirmed with every circumstance which could aggravate the charges made. The captain in a fit of panic left the ship without any substantial excuse, and if it had not been for the good conduct of a young man, his nephew, who, though ordered to leave too, refused out of humanity, there is little doubt that the vessel would have been lost. A very painful impression was produced on the Jeddans while I was there by the news that this

English captain had been sentenced for all punishment by an English court to two years' suspension of his certificate. Indian pilgrims have besides been very roughly treated in Hejaz by the authorities during the last year because they were British subjects, and this without obtaining any redress. Such at least is the gossip of the town. However this may be, it seems to me astonishing that so important a matter as the Indian Haj should be left, as it now is, entirely in the hands of chance.

The Dutch do not so leave the management of their pilgrimage from Java, which, it will be remarked, stands second only to India on my list in respect of numbers. Their policy is a very definite one and seems justified by results. There is no disillusion, they argue, for a Mussulman greater than to have visited Mecca, and they say that a returned hajji is seldom heard to complain in Java of his lot as the subject of a Christian power. Besides the disappointment which all pilgrims are wont to feel who come with exalted hopes and find their holy lands undistinguishable from the other lands of the world, the pilgrim to Mecca certainly has to encounter a series of dangers and annoyances which he cannot but recognize to be the result of Mussulman misgovernment. From the moment of his landing on the holy shore he finds himself beset with dangers. He is fleeced by the Turkish officials, befooled by the religious touts of the towns, and sometimes robbed openly by actual highway robbers. The religious government of the land has no redress to offer him, and the Turkish guardians of the peace who affect to rule are only potent in demanding fees. At every step he is waylaid and tricked and ill-treated. He finds the Hejazi, the keepers of the holy places and privileged ciceroni of the shrines, shrewder as men of business than devout as believers, and he returns to his home a sadder and, the Dutch say, a wiser man. I do not affirm that the Dutch are right; but this is the principle they act on, and they boast of its success.

We in India, as I have said, in our grand careless way, leave all these things to chance. India, nevertheless, still holds the first rank in the Haj, and, all things considered, is now the most important land where the Mohammedan faith is found. In the day of its greatness the Mogul Empire was second to no State in Islam, and though its political power is in abeyance, the religion itself is by no means in decay. India has probably a closer connection at the present moment with Mecca than any other country, and it is looked upon by many there as the Mussulman land of the future. Indeed, it may safely be affirmed that the course of events in India will determine more than anything else the destiny of Mohammedanism in the immediate future of this and the next generation.

The Malays, though holding no very high position in the commonwealth of Islam, are important from their numbers, their commercial prosperity, and, more than all to an European observer, from the fact that so many of them are Dutch subjects. Holland, if any lesson for the future can be learned in history, must in a few years find her fate linked with that of Germany, and so too her colonies. I will not now enlarge upon the prospect thus opened, but it is a suggestive one, and worthy of all possible attention. For the moment the Malays stand rather apart from other pilgrims at the shrines. They boast no great school of theology or particular religious complexion; and as pilgrims they are held in rather low esteem from their penurious ways. But they are a dark element in the future, which it is equally easy to under as to over rate. Originally converted by, and to a certain degree descended from, Arabs, they are, as far as I could learn, followers of the Shafite teaching, and inclined to the broad rather than the narrow ways of Islam. They number, according to the Dutch consular agent at Jeddah, thirty million souls, and are increasing rapidly both in Java and in the other islands of the Malay archipelago.

Another enigma are the Chinese. I saw a few of them in the streets, and made inquiries as to them. But I could gain no certain information. I have heard them estimated as high as twenty millions and as low as five, but it is certain that they are very numerous.[6] They established themselves in China, it is said, about the second century of Islam, and their missionaries were men of Arab race. They are found scattered in groups all over China, but principally inland, and have full enjoyment of their religion, being a united body which is respectable and makes itself respected—so much so that the "Houi-tse," or people of the resurrection, as they are called, are employed in the highest offices of the Chinese State.[7] It is plain, however, that they are hardly at all connected with the modern life of Islam, for it is only within the last few years that any of them have performed the pilgrimage; and if I include them in my lists as Sunites and Shafites it is in default of other classification. They probably hold to the Mussulman world a position analogous in its isolation to that of the Abyssinian Church in Christendom. They too, however, may one day make their existence felt; for China is no dead nation, only asleep. And with them our survey of orthodox Islam ends.

The heretical sects remain to us. Of these the most notable without contestation is the Shiite, or Sect of Ali, which traces its origin to the very day of the Prophet's death, when Abu Bekr was elected Caliph to Ali's exclusion. I will not here renew the arguments urged in this old dispute more than to say that the dispute still exists, though it has long ceased to be the only cause of difference between Shiah and Suni.

Beginning merely as a political schism, the Shiite sect is now distinctly a heresy, and one which has wandered far from the orthodox road. Their principal features of quarrel with the Sunites are—first, a repudiation of the Caliphate and of all hierarchical authority whatsoever; secondly, the admission of a right of free judgment in individual doctors on matters of religion; and thirdly, a general tendency to superstitious beliefs unauthorized by the Koran or by the written testimony of the Prophet's companions. They also—and this is their great doctrinal quarrel with the unitarian Sunites—believe in a series of incarnations of the twelve qualities of God in the persons of the "twelve

Imams," and in the advent of the last of them as a Messiah, or "Mohdy," doctrines which are especially advanced by the Sheykhi school of Shiism and minimized by the Mutesharreh or orthodox. These last matters, however, are rather excrescences than necessary parts of Shiism. They owe their prevalence, without doubt, to the Persian mind, which is equally prone to scepticism and credulity, and where Shiism has always had its stronghold.

The religious constitution of the sect of Ali has been described to me by a member of it who knows Europe well as resembling in its organization the Presbyterian Church of Scotland. That is to say, it acknowledges no head, temporal or spiritual, and each congregation represents a separate unit of authority in itself. There is no such functionary in Persia as Sheykh el Islam, or Grand Mufti, and the Shah claims to be neither Imam nor Caliph. Each Shiite doctor who has taken his degree at Kerbela or Ispahan may deliver his fetwa or opinion on points of doctrine, and the only test of his authority to preach or lead the prayer in mosque is his power of attracting a congregation. It is strange that in a sect which had its origin in an assertion of hereditary right to the Caliphate everything hereditary should be now rigidly excluded.

In theory, I believe the Shias still hold that there is an Imam and Caliph, but they will not tolerate the pretension of any one now in authority to the title, and leave it in abeyance until the advent of the Mohdy, or guide, who is to reunite Islam and restore its fortunes. So much is this the case that, sovereign though he be and absolute master in Persia, the Shah is to the present day looked upon by the Persians as a usurper, and he himself acknowledges the fact in a rather curious ceremony. It is a maxim with Mussulmans of all sects that prayer is not valid if made in another man's house without his permission, and this being so, and the Shah admitting that his palaces of right belong not to himself but to the Mohdy, he is obliged to lease them according to legal form from an alem or mujtahed, acting for the supposed Mohdy, before he can pray in them to his spiritual profit.

It will be readily understood that, with such an organization and with such tendencies to deductive reasoning, a wide basis is given for divergence of opinion among the Shiites, and that while the more highly educated of their mollahs occasionally preach absolute pantheism, others consult the grosser inclinations of the vulgar, and indulge their hearers with the most extravagant tales of miracle and superstition. These are a constant source of mockery to the Sunites. Among the more respectable Shiite beliefs, however, there seems to be a general conviction in Persia that a reform of Islam is at hand, and that a new leader may be expected at any moment and from any quarter, so that enthusiasts are constantly found simulating the gifts of inspiration and affecting a divine mission. The history of the Babites, so well described by M. de Gobineau in his *Religions of Asia*, is a case in point, and similar occurrences are by no means rare in Persia.

I met at Jeddah a highly educated Persian gentleman, who informed me that he had himself been witness when a boy to a religious prodigy, notorious, if I remember rightly, at Tabriz. On that occasion, one of these prophets being condemned to death by the supreme government, was bound to a cross with two of his companions, and after remaining suspended thus for several hours, was fired at by the royal troops. It then happened that, while the companions were dispatched at the first volley, the prophet himself remained unhurt, and, incredible to relate, the cords which bound him were cut by the bullets, and he fell to the ground on his feet. "You Christians," said another Persian gentleman once to me, "talk of your Christ as the Son of God and think it strange, but with us the occurrence is a common one. Believe me we have 'sons of God' in nearly all our villages."

Thus, with the Shiites, extremes meet. No Moslems more readily adapt themselves to the superficial atheisms of Europe than do the Persians, and none are more ardently devout, as all who have witnessed the miracle play of the two Imams will be obliged to admit. Extremes, too, of morality are seen, fierce asceticisms and gross licentiousnesses. By no sect of Islam is the duty of pilgrimage more religiously observed, or the prayers and ablutions required by their rule performed with a stricter ritual. But the very pilgrims who go on foot to Mecca scruple not to drink wine there, and Persian morality is everywhere a byword.

In all these circumstances there is much to fear as well as to hope on the side of the Shiite sect; but their future only indirectly involves that of Islam proper. Their whole census does not probably exceed fifteen millions, and it shows no tendency to increase. Outside Persia we find about one million Iraki Arabs, a few in Syria and Afghanistan, and at most five millions in India. One small group still maintains itself in the neighbourhood of Medina, where it is tolerated rather than acknowledged, and a few Shiites are to be found in most of the large cities of the west, but everywhere the sect of Ali stands apart from and almost in a hostile attitude to the rest of Islam. It is noticeable, however, that within the last fifty years the religious bitterness of Shiite and Sunite is sensibly in decline.

The next most important of the heretical sects is the Abadiyeh. These, according to some, are the religious descendants of the Khawarij, a sect which separated itself from the Caliphate in the time of the Seyid Ali, and, after a severe persecution in Irak, took refuge at last in Oman. Whatever their present doctrines, they seem at first to have been like the Shiites, political schismatics. They maintained that any Mussulman, so long as he was not affected with heresy, might be chosen Imam, and that he might be deposed for heresy or ill-conduct, and indeed that there was no absolute necessity for any Imam at all. They are at present only found in Oman and Zanzibar, where they number, it is said, about four millions. Till as late as the last century the Imamate was an elective office among them, but with the accession of the Abu Said dynasty it became hereditary in that family.[8] They reject all communion with the Sunites, but I have not been able to discover that they hold any doctrines especially offensive to the mass of Moslems. Their differences are mainly negative, and consist in the rejection of Caliphal history and authority later than the reign of Omar, and of a vast number of traditions now incorporated in the Sunite faith.

Allied to them but, as I understood, separate, are the Zeidites of Yemen, who are possibly also descended from the Khawarij. But, as the Zeidites are accustomed to conceal the fact of their heresy and to pass themselves when on pilgrimage as Sunites, I could learn little about them. They were, till ten years ago, independent under the Imams of Sana, and it is certain that they repudiate the Caliphate. In former times, before the first conquest of Arabia by the Turks, these Imams were all powerful in Hejaz, and on the destruction of the Bagdad Caliphate assumed the title of Hami el Harameyn, protector of the holy places. The Turks, however, now occupy Sana, and the office of Imam is in abeyance. The Zeidites can hardly number more than two millions, and their only importance in the future lies in the fact of their geographical proximity to Mecca, and in the fact that their sympathies lie on the side of liberality in opinion and reform in morals. Neither Zeidites nor Abadites have any adherents out of their own countries.

Of the Wahhabites a more detailed account is needed, as although their numbers are small and their political importance less than it formerly was, the spirit of their reform movement still lives and exercises a potent influence on modern Mohammedan ideas. I have described elsewhere[9] the historical vicissitudes of the sect in Arabia, and the decline of its fortunes in Nejd, but a brief recapitulation of these may be allowed me.

The early half of the last century was a period of religious stagnation in Islam, almost as much as it was in Christendom. Faith, morals, and religious practice were at the lowest ebb among Mussulmans, and it seemed to Europeans who looked on as though the faith of Mecca had attained its dotage, and was giving place to a non-curantist infidelity. Politically and religiously the Mussulman world was asleep, when suddenly it awoke, and like a young giant refreshed stood once more erect in Arabia. The reform preached by Abd el Wahhab was radical. He began by breaking with the maxim held by the mass of the orthodox that inquiry on matters of faith was closed. He constituted himself a new mujtahed and founded a new school, neither Hanafite, Malekite, nor Shafite, and called it the school of the Unitarians, Muwaheddin, a name still cherished by the Wahhabites. He rejected positively all traditions but those of the companions of the Prophet, and he denied the claims of any but the first four Caliphs to have been legitimately elected. The Koran was to be the only written law, and Islam was to be again what it had been in the first decade of its existence. He established it politically in Nejd on precisely its old basis at Medina, and sought to extend it over the whole of Arabia, perhaps of the world. I believe it is hardly now recognised by Mohammedans how near Abd el Wahhab was to complete success.

Before the close of the eighteenth century the chiefs of the Ibn Saouds, champions of Unitarian Islam, had established their authority over all Northern Arabia as far as the Euphrates, and in 1808 they took Mecca and Medina. In the meanwhile the Wahhabite doctrines were gaining ground still further afield. India was at one time very near conversion, and in Egypt, and North Africa, and even in Turkey many secretly subscribed to the new doctrines. Two things, however, marred the plan of general reform and prevented its full accomplishment.

In the first place the reform was too completely reactive. It took no account whatever of the progress of modern thought, and directly it attempted to leave Arabia it found itself face to face with difficulties which only political as well as religious success could overcome. It was impossible, except by force of arms, to Arabianise the world again, and nothing less than this was in contemplation. Its second mistake, and that was one that a little of the Prophet's prudence which always went hand in hand with his zeal might have avoided, was a too rigid insistance upon trifles. Abd el Wahhab condemned minarets and tombstones because neither were in use during the first years of Islam. The minarets therefore were everywhere thrown down, and when the holy places of Hejaz fell into the hands of his followers the tombs of saints which had for centuries been revered as objects of pilgrimage were levelled to the ground. Even the Prophet's tomb at Medina was laid waste and the treasures it contained distributed among the soldiers of Ibn Saoud. This roused the indignation of all Islam, and turned the tide of the Wahhabite fortunes. Respectable feeling which had hitherto been on their side now declared itself against them, and they never after regained their position as moral and social reformers.

Politically, too, it was the cause of their ruin. The outside Mussulman world, looking upon them as sacrilegious barbarians, was afraid to visit Mecca, and the pilgrimage declined so rapidly that the Hejazi became alarmed. The source of their revenue they found cut off, and it seemed on the point of ceasing altogether. Then they appealed to Constantinople, urging the Sultan to vindicate his claim to be protector of the holy places. What followed is well known. After the peace of Paris Sultan Mahmud commissioned Mehemet Ali to deliver Mecca and Medina from the Wahhabite heretics, and this he in time effected. The war was carried into Nejd; Deriyeh, their capital, was sacked, and Ibn Saoud himself taken prisoner and decapitated in front of St. Sophia's at Constantinople. The movement of reform in Islam was thus put back for, perhaps, another hundred years.

Still the seed cast by Abd el Wahhab has not been entirely without fruit. Wahhabism, as a political regeneration of the world, has failed, but the spirit of reform has remained. Indeed, the present unquiet attitude of expectation in Islam has been its indirect result. Just as the Lutheran reformation in Europe, though it failed to convert the Christian Church, caused its real reform, so Wahhabism has produced a real desire for reform if not yet reform itself in Mussulmans. Islam is no longer asleep, and were another and a wiser Abd el Wahhab to appear, not as a heretic, but in the body of the Orthodox sect, he might play the part of Loyola or Borromeo with success.

The present condition of the Wahhabites as a sect is

one of decline. In India, and I believe in other parts of Southern Asia, their missionaries still make converts and their preachers are held in high esteem. But at home in Arabia their zeal has waxed cold, giving place to liberal ideas which in truth are far more congenial to the Arabian mind. The Ibn Saoud dynasty no longer holds the first position in Nejd, and Ibn Rashid who has taken their place, though nominally a Wahhabite, has little of the Wahhabite fanaticism. He is in fact a popular and national rather than a religious leader, and though still designated at Constantinople as a pestilent heretic, is counted as their ally by the more liberal Sunites. It is probable that he would not withhold his allegiance from a Caliph of the legitimate house of Koreysh. But this, too, is beyond the subject of the present chapter.

With the Wahhabites, then, our census of Islam closes. It has given us, as I hope, a fairly accurate view of the forces which make up the Mohammedan world, and though the enumeration of these cannot but be dull work, I do not think it will have been work done in vain. Without it indeed it would be almost impossible to make clear the problem presented to us by modern Islam or guess its solution. More interesting matter, however, lies before us, and in my next chapter I propose to introduce my reader to that burning question of the day in Asia, the Caliphate, and explain the position of the House of Othman towards the Mohammedan world.

NOTES

[1]   The following is a formula of the faith:—

1. That thou believest in God, the one God and none other with Him, and that thou believest that Mohammed is His servant and His Apostle.

2. That thou believest in the Holy Angels and the Holy Books, the Pentateuch, the Psalms, the Gospels and the Koran.

3. That thou believest in the Last Day, and in the Providence of God both for good and for evil.

[2]   The Hanbali ritual is now almost entirely confined to Medina and Kasim in Central Arabia.

[3]   This was written before the events of last September, which have given a new impulse to liberalism in Egypt, though it has taken the direction of Mohammedan thought there out of the hands of the Khedive.

[4]   The exact composition of the Azhar university is as follows. Of the five hundred and odd sheykhs or professors, two hundred are Shafite, two hundred Malekite, one hundred Hanefite, and five Hanbalite. Each of these sections has a supreme sheykh, chosen by itself, whose fetwa on questions concerning the school is decisive. There is, moreover, a Sheykh el Islam, also elected, who decides religious questions of general importance, and a Grand Mufti appointed by the Government who gives fetwas on matters of law. The latter is Hanefite, the former at the present moment Shafite, as are the bulk of the students. These number about fifteen hundred.

[5]   It is the secret of the rapid conversions in ancient days among the poor of the Roman and Persian Empires, and it is the secret of those now taking place among the low-caste Indians.

[6] The Mohammedan revolts in Yunan and Kashgar, repressed with great ferocity by the Chinese, have in late years temporarily diminished the Mohammedan census; but there seems good reason to believe that they are making steady progress in the Empire.

[7] Compare M. Huc's account of their origin.

[8] Compare Dr. Badger's *History of Oman* and Sale's *Koran*.

[9] Lady Anne Blunt's *Pilgrimage to Nejd*. Appendix.

II

The Modern Question
of the Caliphate

About the year 1515 of our era (921 of the Hejra), Selim
I., Padishah of the Ottoman Turks and Emperor of
Constantinople, finding himself the most powerful prince
of his day in Islam, and wishing still further to consolidate
his rule, conceived the idea of reviving in his own person
the extinct glories of the Caliphate. He had more than
one claim to be considered their champion by orthodox
Mohammedans, for he was the grandson of that Mahomet
II. who had finally extinguished the Roman Empire of the
East, and he had himself just ended a successful campaign
against the heretical Shah of Persia, head of the Sect of
Ali. His only rivals among Sunite princes were the Sultan
el Hind, or, as we call him, the Great Mogul, the Sultan
el Gharb, or Emperor of Morocco, and the Mameluke
Sultan of Egypt, then known to the world as *par excellence*
the Sultan.

With the two former, as rulers of what were remote
lands of Islam, Selim seems to have troubled himself little;
but he made war on Egypt. In 1516 he invaded Syria, its
outlying province, and in 1517 he entered Cairo. There he

made prisoner the reigning Mameluke, Kansaw el Ghouri, and had him publicly beheaded, or according to another account, received his head from a soldier, who had killed him where he lay on the ground after falling (for the Sultan was an old man) from his horse. He then, in virtue of a very doubtful cession made to him of his rights by one Motawakkel Ibn Omar el Hakim, a descendant of the house of Abbas, whom he found living as titular Caliph in Cairo, took to himself the following style and title: Sultan es Salatin, wa Hakan el Hawakin, Malek el Bahreyn, wa Hami el Barreyn, Khalifeh Rasul Allah, Emir el Mumenin, wa Sultan, wa Khan—titles which may be thus interpreted: King of Kings and Lord of Lords, Monarch of the two seas (the Mediterranean and the Red Sea), and Protector of the two lands (Hejaz and Syria, the holy lands of Islam), Successor of the Apostle of God, Prince of the Faithful, and Emperor. It is said that he first had the satisfaction of hearing his name mentioned in the public prayers as Caliph when he visited the great mosque of Zacharias at Aleppo on his return northwards in 1519.[10]

Such, in a few words, is historically the origin of the modern Caliphate, and such are the titles now borne by Selim's descendant, Abd el Hamid. It is difficult at this distance of time, and in the absence of detailed contemporary narratives, to do more than guess the effect on Mussulmans of his day of Selim's religious pretensions. To all alike, friends as well as foes, he must in the first instance have appeared as an usurper, for before him no man not of the house of Koreysh, and so a kinsman of their Prophet, had ever claimed to be his spiritual heir. Indeed, it was a maxim with all schools of theology of all ages that descent from the Koreysh was the first title to the Caliphate; but we may reasonably suppose that within the limits of his own dominions, and even to the mass of the vulgar beyond them, the Ottoman Emperor's sublime proceedings met with approval.

Selim was a portentous figure in Islam; and the splendour of his apparition in the north dazzled the eyes of all. Mussulmans must have seen in him and his house the restorers of their political fortunes and the champion of their religion against Christendom; and a departure from established rule in his favour may well have seemed justified to pious persons as the best hope for the future of their creed. Selim was already temporal lord of the greater part of Islam, and he might be expected thus to restore the spiritual sovereignty also. Besides, to the ears of Mussulmans of the sixteenth century, the Caliphal title was no longer a familiar sound, and the title of Sultan which Selim already bore was that of the highest temporal authority they knew.

The Caliphate, if it existed at all, was in the modern world a less imposing name than the Sultanate; and the two had since the destruction of Bagdad become confused, as they still remain, in men's minds who do not any more now make common use of the older title. Thus it was not difficult for the new Sultan of Damascus and Cairo and Medina to impose himself on the multitude—not merely as heir to the Caliphal possessions, but to the title also of the Caliphs and their spiritual rank. Advantage, too, seems to have been taken in the first instance, as it has been subsequently, of the accidental resemblance of name between Othman, Selim's ancestor, and Othman the third Caliph. The vulgar ear caught the sound as one familiar to it, and was satisfied, for there is all the world in a name.

With the Ulema, however, it was necessary to be more precise; and we know that the question of the Ottoman right to the spiritual succession of the Prophet was one long and hotly debated in the schools. Tradition was formal on the point of excluding aliens to the Koreysh from this its legal inheritance, for Mohammed himself had repeatedly distinguished his own tribe as being the sole heirs to his authority; nor would any doctor of the specially Arabian schools listen to a departure from ideas so absolute. The Hanefite school, however, representing those chiefly interested in accepting the Ottoman pretension, undertook its legal defence, and succeeded, in spite of the one great obstacle of birth, in making out a very tolerable case for themselves and the Beni Othman—a case which, in the absence of any rival candidate to oppose to them, has since been tacitly accepted by the majority of the Sunite Ulema.

The difficulty, however, was in practice settled by a compromise, and the dispute itself had long been forgotten by all but the learned, until within the present generation its arguments were once more dragged out publicly to serve a political purpose. The Hanefite arguments are on this account interesting, and I have been at pains to ascertain and understand them; but perhaps before I state them in detail it will be best first briefly to run over the Caliphal history of an earlier age and describe the state of things which Selim's act superseded.

Orthodox Mussulman writers recognize four distinct phases which the office of Khalifeh has undergone, and four distinct periods of its history. The word Khalifeh, derived from the Arabic root *khalafa*, to "leave behind," signifies literally one left behind, and in the legal sense the relict or successor of the prophet and heir to his temporal and spiritual power.

The *first* historical phase noticed is one of pure theocracy, in which the Caliph or successor of Mohammed was saint as well as priest and king, and was to a certain extent inspired. It lasted thirty years only, and is represented by the four great Caliphs—Abu Bekr, Omar, Othman, and Ali—who receive from the faithful when they speak of them the title of Seydna, or Our Lord.

The *second* phase, which lasted nearly six hundred years, is that of the Arabian monarchy, in which the Caliphate took the shape of hereditary temporal dominion. Its representatives are neither saints nor doctors of the law, and stand on a quite different footing from those who precede them. They begin with Mawiyeh ibn Ommiyah, founder of the Ommiad dynasty, and end with Mostasem Billah, the last Sultan of the Abbasides.

The *third* period is a phase of temporal inter-regnum during which for nearly three hundred years the Khalifeh exercised no sovereign rights, and resided as a spiritual chief only, or as we should now say Sheykh el Islam, at Cairo. The temporal authority of Islam, which is theoretically supposed to have been continued without break even during this period, was then in delegation with the Memluk Sultans of Egypt and other Mussulman princes.

The *last* phase is that of the Ottoman Caliphate.

As nearly all modern arguments respecting the Caliphate appeal to examples in the earliest period, it will be well to consider the origin of its institution and the political basis of Islam itself. Mohammedan doctors affirm that the Apostle of God, Mohammed (on whose name be peace), when he fled from Mecca, did so not as a rebellious citizen but as a pretender to authority. He was by birth a prince of the princely house of the Koreysh, itself the noblest tribe of Hejaz, and his grandfather had been supreme ruler in Mecca. He established himself, therefore, with his companions in exile as head of an independent political community, following in this the ancient custom of Arabia where sections constantly cut themselves off from the parent tribe and form new nations under the separate leadership of one or another member of their princely families. Islam, therefore, was from its commencement a political as well as a religious body, and while Mohammed preached to his disciples as a prophet, he also gave laws to them as their king and governor. He was their Imam, the leader of their prayer, and he was their Emir and Kadi, prince and magistrate. Thus the supreme temporal and spiritual authority became linked, and Islam was from its beginning a nation no less than a church.

As long as Mohammed lived, this state of things remained unquestioned, and difficulties began only at his death. It is a point which has been much disputed what were the prophet's intentions regarding this event. In early times the sect of Ali maintained that he had appointed his son-in-law his heir, and others have held that Abu Bekr had the nomination; but Sunites are now mostly agreed that no individual appointment was made, and that the choice of a successor was left to be decided by election. In any case the procedure followed by Mohammed's bereaved followers was elective, and its details were in strict accordance with that Arabian custom on which the Koranic law is mainly built.

Now, in an Arab tribe, when the Sheykh dies, the elders of the tribe, heads of its great houses and sections, assemble in one of their number's tent and, sitting in a circle, discuss the subject of his succession. Theoretically, the choice of a successor is open to any one of them, for the tribe, however large, is all one great family, descended from a common ancestor, and though no one from without could be admitted to the supreme rule, any one from within the tribe can hold office. But in practice the choice is limited to a few persons. The reverence of the Arabs for blood, and for selected strains of blood, prevent them, except in very exceptional cases, from changing the dynasty of their rulers. If the dead man has left behind him a son of full age and respectable qualities, he will, without dispute, be acknowledged Sheykh. If not, an uncle, a nephew, or a cousin will be chosen. Only in extreme circumstances of general danger, or of failure of heirs male, can the member of a new family reasonably aspire to power. Moreover, there is no uniform law of election. The meeting does not pretend to give a right, only to confirm one; for the right lies not with the electors but with him who can maintain his election. There is, therefore, no formal system of voting, but the elders having ascertained who among the dead man's relations commands the strongest following, proceed to acknowledge him by the ceremony of giving him their hands. He then becomes their Sheykh. It sometimes happens, however, that parties are so evenly divided between rival leaders that the tribe divides, one section going this way and the other that, until one of the leaders gives in his submission; otherwise the quarrel is decided by the sword.

All these features of the Arabian tribal system of succession may be noticed in the first elections to the Caliphate. As soon as it was known that Mohammed was indeed dead, a conclave composed of the elders and chief men of Islam, self-constituted and recognizing no special popular mandate, assembled in the house of Omar ibn el Khattub. This conclave is known to jurists as the *Ahl el helli wa el agde*, the people of the loosing and the knotting, because they assumed the duty of solving the knotty question of succession. A nice point had to be decided, just such a one as has in all ages been the cause of civil war in Arabia. The Prophet had left no son, but more than one near relation. Moreover, at that moment the new nation of Islam was in danger of internal disruption, and the religious and the civil elements in it were on the point of taking up arms against each other. The two chief candidates were Ali ibn Abutaleb and Abu Bekr, the one son-in-law and cousin and the other father-in-law of Mohammed—Ali represented the civil, Abu Bekr the religious party; and as it happened that the latter party was predominant at Medina, it was on Abu Bekr that the choice fell. He was recognized as head of the more powerful faction, and the chiefs gave him their hands; while civil war was only prevented by the magnanimous submission of Ali.

This form of succession is held by most Sunite doctors to be the authentic form intended by the Prophet, nor did the three following elections differ from it in any essential point. It is only noticed that Abu Bekr designated Omar as the most fitting person to succeed him, and so in a measure directed the choice of the Ahl el agde. The Caliph was in each instance elected by the elders at Medina, and the choice confirmed by its general acknowledgment elsewhere.

In the time of Ali, however, a new principle began to make its appearance, which foreshadowed a change in the nature of the Caliphate. The election of Abu Bekr, as I have said, was determined by the predominant religious feeling of the day. He was the holiest man in Islam, and his government was throughout strictly theocratic. He not only administered the religious law, but was its interpreter and architect. He sat every day in the *mejlis*, or open court of justice, and decided there questions of divinity as well as of jurisprudence. He publicly led the prayer in the Mosque, expounded the Koran, and preached every Friday from the pulpit. He combined in his person all the functions now divided between the Sheykh el Islam, the grand Mufti, and the executive authorities. He was king and priest and magistrate, doctor of civil and religious law, and supreme referee on all matters whether of opinion or practice; he was, in a word, the Pope of Islam. Nor did his three successors abate anything of Abu Bekr's pretensions. The only power they delegated was the command of the Mussulman armies, which were then overrunning the world, and the government of the provinces these had conquered.

Ali, however, when he at last succeeded to the Caliphate, found himself opposed by the very party whose candidate he had once been, and this party had gathered strength in the interval. With the conquest of the world worldly ideas had filled the hearts of Mussulmans, and a strong reaction also had set in in favour of those specially national ideas of Arabia which religious fervour had hitherto held in check. It was natural, indeed inevitable, that this should be the case, for many conquered nations had embraced the faith of Islam, and, as Mussulmans, had become the equals of their conquerors, so that what elements of pride existed in these found their gratification in ideas of race and birth rather than of religion, ideas which the conquered races could not share, and which were the special inheritance of Arabia.

The national party, then, had been reinforced, at the expense of the religious, among the Koreysh, who were still at the head of all the affairs of State. Their leader was Mawiyeh Ibn Ommiyeh, a man of distinguished ability and of that charm of manner which high-born Arabs know so well how to use to their political ends. He had for some years been Governor of Syria, and was more popular there than the pious Ali; and Syria, though not yet the nominal, was already the real seat of the Mussulman Government. Mawiyeh therefore refused to accept Ali's election at Medina as valid, and finding himself supported by a rival Ahl el agde at Damascus, made that appeal to the sword which Arabian usage sanctions as the ultimate right of all pretenders.

Religious writers agree in condemning Mawiyeh for his revolt; and while his succession to Ali is accepted as legal, they place him on quite a different level from the four Caliphs who preceded him. In Mawiyeh they see fulfilled that prediction of their Prophet which announced that Islam should be ruled for thirty years by an Imam, and ever after by a King. Mawiyeh is, indeed, the type of all the later Mohammedan Emperors. According to canon law, the head of the State is also head of the religion; but Mawiyeh ceased to exercise religious functions in person. These, unlike his predecessors, he delegated to others, and neither led the prayer nor preached; nor was he held to be either the best or the most learned man in Islam, as Abu Bekr and the rest had been. Moreover—and this is the chief point noticed regarding him—he introduced the system of dynastic heredity into the Caliphate, nominating his son Yezid his successor in his own lifetime. The change, advantageous as it was politically, is regarded as a religious falling off. Henceforth the Caliphs, whether of the Ommiad or afterwards of the Abbaside families, were not in reality elected, though the form of confirmation by the Ulema was gone through; and they affected to succeed by right of birth, not by the voice of the people.

During the whole period of the Arabian Caliphate we only notice one Prince of the Faithful who busied himself much with religious learning, and few who personally exercised the magisterial functions. Only once we read of an Abbaside Caliph insisting on his right of leading the prayer, and this was probably the effect of an accidental jealousy. As a rule the temporal government of Islam was intrusted to a *Sadrazzam*, or Grand Vizier, the spiritual duty of prayer to a *Naib*, or deputy Imam, and the elaboration or interpretation of law and doctrine to such Ulema or Mujtaheddin as could command a following. The character of the Khalifeh, however, was still essentially sacred. He was of the Koreysh and of the blood of the Prophet, and so was distinct from the other princes of the world. As their political power decayed, the Abbasides fell indeed into the hands of adventurers who even occasionally used them as puppets for their own ambitious ends; but the office was respected, and neither the Kurdish Saladdin, nor Togral Bey, nor Malek Shah, nor any of the Seljukian Emirs el Amara dared meddle personally with the title of Caliph.

The Ommiad dynasty, founded by Mawiyeh, reigned at Damascus eighty-five years, and was then succeeded on a new appeal to the sword in A.D. 750 by the descendants of another branch of the Koreysh—the Beni Abbas—who transferred the capital of Islam to Bagdad, and survived as temporal sovereigns there for five hundred years.

This second period of Islam, though containing her greatest glories and her highest worldly prosperity, is held to be less complete by divines than the first thirty years which had preceded it. Islam was no longer one. To say nothing of the Persian and Arabian schisms, the orthodox world itself was divided, and rival Caliphs had established themselves independently in Spain and Egypt. Moreover, during the last two centuries the temporal power of the Caliphs was practically in delegation to the Seljuk Turks, who acted as mayors of the palace, and their spiritual power was unsupported by any show of sanctity or learning. It was terminated forcibly by the pagan Holagu, who at the head of the Mongols sacked Bagdad in 1258.

The third period of Caliphal history saw all temporal power wrested from the Caliphs. Islam, on the destruction of the Arabian monarchy, resolved itself into a number of separate States, each governed by its own Bey or Sultan, who in his quality of temporal prince was head also of religion within his own dominions. The Mongols, converted to the Faith of Mecca, founded a Mohammedan empire in the east; the Seljuk Turks, replaced by the Ottoman, reigned in Asia Minor; the Barbary States had their own rulers; and Egypt was governed by that strange dynasty of slaves, the Mameluke Sultans. Nowhere was a supreme temporal head of Islam to be seen, and the name of Khalifeh as that of a reigning sovereign ceased any longer to be heard of in the world. Only the nominal succession of the Prophet was obscurely preserved at Cairo, whither the survivors of the family of Abbas had betaken themselves on the massacre of their house at Bagdad.

It is difficult to ascertain the precise position of these titular Caliphs under the Mameluke monarchy in Egypt. That they were little known to the world in general is certain; and one is sometimes tempted to suspect the complete authenticity of the succession preserved through them. Contemporary Christian writers do not mention them, and it is evident from Sir John Mandeville and others that in Egypt the Egyptian Sultan himself was talked of as head of the Mussulman religion. I have heard their position compared with that of the present Sheykhs el Islam at Constantinople—that is to say, they were appointed by the Sultan, and were made use of by him as a means of securing Mussulman allegiance—and I believe this to have been all their real status. They are cited, however, as in some sense sovereigns by Hanefite teachers, whose argument it is that the succession of the Prophet has never lapsed, or Islam been without a recognized temporal head. The Sultans, neither of Egypt nor of India, nor till Selim's time of the Turkish Empire, ever claimed for themselves the title of Khalifeh, nor did the Sherifal family of Mecca, who alone of them might have claimed it legally as Koreysh. Neither did Tamerlane nor any of the Mussulman Mongols who reigned at Bagdad. The fact is, we may assume the Caliphate was clean forgotten at the time Selim bethought him of it as an instrument of power.

It must, then, have been an interesting and startling novelty with Mussulmans to hear of this new pretender to the ancient dignity—interesting, because the name Khalifeh was connected with so many of the bygone glories of Islam; startling, because he who claimed it seemed by birth incapable of doing so. The Hanefite Ulema, however, as I have said, undertook Selim's defence, or rather that of his successors, for Selim himself died not a year afterwards, and succeeded in proving, to the satisfaction of the majority of Sunites, that the house of Othman had a good and valid title to the rank they had assumed. Their chief arguments were as follows. The house of Othman, they asserted, ruled spiritually by—

1. *The right of the sword*, that is to say, the *de facto* possession of the sovereign title. It was argued that, the Caliphate being a necessity (and this all orthodox Mussulmans admit), it was also necessary that the *de facto* holder of the title should be recognized as legally the Caliph, *until a claimant with a better title should appear*. Now the first qualification of a claimant was that he should claim, and the second that he should be supported by a party; and Selim had both claimed the Caliphate and supported his pretensions at the head of an army. He had challenged the world to produce a rival, and no rival had been found— none, at least, which the Hanefite school acknowledged, for the Sultan of Morocco they had never accepted, and

the last descendant of the Abbasides had waived his rights. In support of the proposition that the sword could give a title they cited the examples of Mawiyeh, who thus established his right against the family of Ali, and of Abu el Abbas, who had thus established his against that of Mawiyeh.

2. *Election*, that is the sanction of a legal body of Elders. It was argued that, as the Ahl el agde had been removed from Medina to Damascus, and from Damascus to Bagdad, and from Bagdad to Cairo, so it had been once more legally removed from Cairo to Constantinople. Selim had brought with him to St. Sophia's some of the Ulema of the Azhar mosque in Cairo, and these, in conjunction with the Turkish Ulema, had elected him or ratified his election. A form of election is to the present day observed at Constantinople in token of this right; and each new Sultan of the house of Othman, as he succeeds to the temporal sovereignty of Turkey, must wait before being recognized as Caliph till he has received the sword of office at the hands of the Ulema. This ceremony it is customary to perform in the mosque of Ayub.

3. *Nomination*. Sultan Selim, as has been already said, obtained from Mutawakkel, a descendant of the Abbasides and himself titularly Caliph, a full cession of all the Caliphal rights of that family. The fact, as far as it goes, is historical, and the only flaw in the argument would seem to be that Mutawakkel had no right thus to dispose of a title to an

alien, which was his own only in virtue of his birth. The case, indeed, was very much as though the Emperor of Germany, having possessed himself of London, should obtain from Don Carlos a cession of the throne of Spain; or as though Napoleon should have got such a cession of the Papacy, in 1813, from Pius VII. Still it is insisted upon strongly by the Hanefite divines as giving a more permanent dynastic title than either of the previous pleas. As a precedent for nomination they cite the act of Abu Bekr, who on his death-bed recommended Omar as his successor in the Caliphate.

4. *The guardianship of the two shrines*, that is to say of Mecca and Jerusalem, but especially of Mecca. It has been asserted by some of the Ulema, and it is certainly a common opinion at the present day, that the sovereignty of Hejaz is in itself sufficient title to the Caliphate. It seems certainly to have been so considered in the first age of Islam, and many a bloody war was then fought for the right of protecting the Beyt Allah; but the connection of Hejaz with the Empire of the Caliphs has been too often broken to make this a very tenable argument. In the tenth century it was held by the Karmathian heretics, in the thirteenth by the Imams of Sana, and for seven years in the present century by the Wahhabis. Still the *de facto* sovereignty of the Harameyn, or two shrines, was one of Selim's pleas; and it is one which has reappeared in modern arguments respecting the Caliphal rights of his descendants.

5. *Possession of the Amanat* or sacred relics. This last was a plea addressed to the vulgar rather than to the learned; but it is one which cannot be passed by unnoticed here, for it exercises a powerful influence at the present day over the ignorant mass of Mussulmans. It was asserted, and is still a pious belief, that from the sack of Bagdad, in 1258, certain relics of the Prophet and his companions were saved and brought to Cairo, and thence transferred by Selim to Constantinople. These were represented to constitute the Imperial insignia of office, and their possession to give a title to the Caliphal succession. They consisted of the cloak of the Prophet borne by his soldiers as a standard, of some hairs from his beard, and of the sword of Omar. The vulgar believe them to be still preserved in the mosque of Ayub; and though the Ulema no longer insist on their authenticity, they are often referred to as an additional test of the Sultan's right.

Such, then, were the arguments of the Hanefite school, who defended Selim's claim, and such they are with regard to his successors of the house of Othman. By the world at large they seem to have been pretty generally accepted, the more so as the Turkish Sultans, having only a political end in view, were satisfied with their formal recognition by their own subjects, and did not bring the question to an issue with their independent neighbours. Neither the Mogul Emperors at Delhi nor the Sheriffs of Morocco were called upon to acknowledge temporal or spiritual supremacy in the Ottoman Sultans, nor did these affect an every-day use of the ancient title they had assumed.

In India the head of the house of Othman was still known to Moslems as Padishah or Sultan er Roum, the Roman Emperor, the most powerful of Mussulman princes, but not in any special manner the head of their religion, certainly not their sovereign. The Ulema, indeed, such as were Hanefites, admitted him to be legally Khalifeh; but many of the Shafite school denied this, pleading still that as an alien to the Koreysh his claim was illegal, while to the ignorant mass of the people out of his dominions his spiritual title remained almost unknown. The Sultans themselves were doubtless to blame for this, seeing that the spiritual functions of their new office were left almost entirely unperformed. For it cannot be too strongly insisted on that the assumption of the Caliphate was to the house of Othman only a means to an end, viz. the consolidation of its worldly power upon a recognized basis, and that, once that end obtained, the temporal dignity of Sultan was all that they really considered. Thus they never sought to exercise the right appertaining to the Caliphal office of appointing Naibs, or Deputy Imams, in the lands outside their dominions, or to interfere with doctrinal matters at home, except where such might prejudice the interests of their rule. With regard to these, the theologians of Constantinople, having satisfactorily settled the Caliphal dispute, and pronounced the house of Othman for ever heirs to the dignity they had assumed, were recommended by the head of the State to busy themselves no further with doctrinal matters, and to consider the *ijtahad*, or development of new dogma, altogether closed for the future in their schools. Soliman the Magnificent, Selim's heir, especially insisted upon this. He had already promulgated a series of decrees affecting the civil administration of his empire, which he had declared to be immutable; and an immutability, too, in dogma he thought would still further secure the peace and stability of his rule. Nor did he meet with aught but approval here from the Hanefite divines.

The Turkish Ulema, ever since their first appearance in the Arabian schools in the eleventh century, finding themselves at a disadvantage through their ignorance of the sacred language, and being constitutionally adverse to intellectual effort, had maintained the proposition that mental repose was the true feature of orthodoxy, and in their *fetwas* had consistently relied on authority and rejected original argument. They therefore readily seconded the Sultan in his views. Argument on first principles was formally forbidden in the schools; and for the interpretation of existing law two offices were invented—the one for dogmatic, the other for practical decisions, those of the Sheykh el Islam and the Great Mufti. This closing of doctrinal inquiry by the Ottoman Sultans, and the removal of the seat of supreme spiritual government from the Arabian atmosphere of Cairo to the Tartar atmosphere of the Bosphorus, was the direct and immediate cause of the religious stagnation which Islam suffered from so conspicuously in the seventeenth and eighteenth centuries.

We have now brought the history of the Caliphate down to the period described in the last chapter as one of intellectual torpor for Islam. It was a lethargy from which there seemed no awakening, and which to contemporaries, Voltaire among the rest, seemed closely approximating to the death of unbelief. In spite of Soliman's eternal arrangements, the temporal power of the house of Othman was wofully diminished, and the spiritual prestige of the Sultans was gone with Mussulmans. By the middle of the last century the title of Caliph, even in their own dominions, was all but forgotten, and the Court of Constantinople was become a byword for its vice and infidelity. It can therefore be well imagined that the awakening of religious feeling, which I also described as having been produced by the Wahhabite movement, especially menaced the Sultan in his Caliphal pretensions. By the beginning of the present century the serious world of Islam was already ripening for a change, and the title of the Caliphate seemed open to whoever should re-invent and prove himself worthy to wear it. Two men certainly then dreamed of its acquisition, both men of supreme genius, and holding the elements of success in their hands. Nor can it be doubted that either of them would have achieved his ambition but for the appearance against them of a material power greater than their own, and which then, for the first time, began to make itself felt as paramount in Asia. That power was England, and the ambitions she thwarted there were those of Bonaparte and Mehemet Ali.

It is not, I believe, sufficiently understood how vast a scheme was overthrown by the Battle of the Nile. Napoleon's mind was formed for dominion in the East, and where he failed in Europe he would have infallibly succeeded in Asia. There little policies are useless, and great ones root themselves in a congenial soil; and he was possessed with an idea which must have flourished. His English opponents, judging him only by the scale of their own thoughts, credited him with the inferior design of invading India through Persia, and called it a mad one; but India was, in fact, a small part only of his programme. When he publicly pronounced the Kelemat at Cairo, and professed the faith of Islam, he intended to be its Head, arguing rightly that what had been possible three hundred years before to Selim was possible also then to him. Nor would the Mussulman world have been much more astonished in 1799 at being asked to accept a Bonaparte for Caliph, than it was in 1519 at being asked to accept an Ottoman. With Napoleon's genius for war, and but for the disastrous sea fight on the Nile, all this might have been, and more; and it is conceivable that Europe, taken in reverse by a great Moslem multitude, might have suffered worse disasters than any the actual Napoleonic wars procured her, while a more durable empire might have been founded on the Nile or Bosphorus than the Bonapartes were able to establish on the Seine. As it was, it was an episode and no more, useful only to the few who saw it near enough to admire and understand.[11]

Among these who saw and understood was Mehemet Ali, the Albanian adventurer, who undertook the government of Egypt when England restored it to the Porte. Bonaparte from the first was his model, and he inherited from him this vision of a new Caliphate, the greatest of the Napoleonic ideas, and worked persistently to realize it. He was within an ace of succeeding. In 1839 Mehemet Ali had Mecca, Cairo, and Jerusalem in his hands, and he had defeated the Sultan at Konia, and was advancing through Asia Minor on Constantinople. There, without doubt, he would have proclaimed himself Caliph, having all the essential elements of the Sultan's admitted right on which to found a new claim.

Nor is it probable that he would have found much religious opposition to the realization of his scheme from the Turkish Ulema. These, already alarmed by Sultan Murad's administrative reforms, would hardly have espoused the Sultan's defence with any vigour; and though Mehemet Ali himself was open to a charge of latitudinarianism, he had the one great claim upon orthodox Islam of having delivered the Holy Cities of Mecca and Medina from the Wahhabis. The house of Othman, indeed, at this time had begun to stink—not only in the nostrils of the outside world, but in that of the Hanefite school itself; and as these had formerly accepted Selim, so they might very well, in 1839, have accepted Mehemet Ali. But this attempt, too, was stopped by England in pursuance of a policy which it is difficult now not to regret. The too venturous Arnaout was sent back to his vice-royalty in Egypt, and the House of Othman was entrusted with a new lease of spiritual sovereignty, if not yet of spiritual power.

The reigns of Abd el Mejid and of Abd el Aziz are remarkable with Mussulmans as having witnessed a complete dissociation of interests between the Imperial Government and the Old Hanefite school of Ulema. I have no space here to discuss the nature of the reforms attempted and partly effected in the Ottoman Empire between the years 1839 and 1869 as a concession to the clamour of Europe. They were instituted not by and through religion, as they should have been, but in defiance of it, and so failed to find acceptance anywhere with religious people. All changes so attempted must fail in Islam because they have in them the inevitable vice of illegality, and I hope to have an opportunity of explaining later the manner in which alone a true reform can hope to find acceptance. For the present I only note the promulgation of the Hatti Humayoum and its kindred decrees as points in the history of the Ottoman Caliphate's decline, and as direct reasons for the reactionary change of front which we now witness in the policy of Constantinople.

Abd el Mejid for his ill-judged attempts gained with Mussulmans the name of an unbeliever, and his son was deposed in the way we all know as a breaker of the religious law. For a moment, however, Abd el Aziz seems to have seen the true nature of his position and to have had some idea of the *role* required of him, as the following incident will show. It marks at any rate the epoch pretty exactly when a revival of the Sultan's spiritual pretensions, as a settled policy, was first resolved on in Turkey. The circumstances have been narrated to me as follows:—

Quite in the early days of Abd el Aziz's reign a certain statesman, a man of original genius and profoundly versed in the knowledge both of Europe and of the East, and especially of the religious history of Islam, came to Constantinople. He was a friend of Rushdi Pasha, then the Grand Vizier, and of others of the party of Young Turkey, men who were seeking by every means, fair and foul, to reorganize and strengthen the central authority of the Empire. To these, and subsequently, in an interview, to the Sultan himself, he urged the advantage which might accrue to the Ottoman Government both as a means of controlling the provinces and as a weapon against European diplomacy if the spiritual authority of the Sultan as Caliph were put more prominently forward. He suggested especially to Abd el Aziz that his real strength lay in the reorganization not of his temporal but of his spiritual forces; and he expressed his wonder that so evident a source of strength had been so little drawn on. He pointed out the importance of the Mussulman populations outside the Empire to the Sultan, and urged that these should be brought as much as possible within the sphere of Constantinople influence. The Barbary States, Mussulman India, and Central Asia might thus become to all intents and purposes, save that of tribute, subjects of the Porte.

In early times it had been a duty of the Caliphs to appoint in all the provinces of Islam Imams or deputies to represent their spiritual authority, and it was suggested that these should once more be appointed. An Imam, or leader of their public prayer, is a necessity with orthodox Mussulmans, and in default of legal appointment from the Caliph, who is himself the supreme Imam, the faithful had been constrained to apply either to the local governments for such appointment or to elect the functionary themselves. This they acknowledged to be illegal, and would willingly revert to the more legitimate system; while the re-establishment of such a hierarchy would bring an enormous accession of spiritual power to Constantinople. It was also shown to Abd el Aziz how all-important Arabia was to his position, and how greatly the means of influence there had been neglected.

I am informed by one present at this interview that Abd el Aziz was not only delighted at the idea, but profoundly astonished. He seems to have had no notion previously either of the historical dignity of the spiritual office he held nor of its prerogatives, and for a while his thoughts were turned in the direction pointed out to him. He sent for the chief Ulema and asked them if all he heard was true; and, when he found their ideas to be entirely in unison with the advice just given him, he commissioned the Sheykh el Islam to push forward the doctrine of his spiritual leadership by all the means in his power. Missionaries were consequently despatched to every part of the Mussulman world, and especially to India and the Barbary States, to explain the Hanefite dogma of the Caliphate; and though at first these met with little success they eventually gained their object in those countries where believers were obliged to live under infidel rule, so much so that in a few years the Ottoman Caliphate became once more a recognized "question" in the schools. They were aided in this by a powerful instrument, then first employed in Turkey, the press.[12] A newspaper in Arabic called the *Jawaib* was subsidized at Constantinople under the direction of one Achmet Faris, a convert to Islam and a man of great literary ability and knowledge of Arabic, who already had views on the subject of the Caliphate; and this organ henceforth consistently advocated the new policy of the Ulema.

The official clique in Stamboul were, however, at that time still intent on other projects, and only half understood the part to be played by religion in their scheme of administrative reform for the Empire. Besides—and this was the chief hindrance to the Ulema—Abd el Aziz was not a man capable of seriously carrying out a great political idea, being little else than a man of pleasure. He and his government consequently soon drifted back into the groove of his predecessors' material policy, which relied for its strength on the physical force of arms, foreign loans, and the intrigues of officials. The only practical action taken by Ottoman ministers in the line indicated were the twin crusades proclaimed against the Wahhabis of Hasa and the heretical Imams of Sana. But the Hanefite Ulema were not thus to be satisfied. They had determined on carrying out the idea they had adopted, and on forcing the Sultan to put himself openly at the head of a religious and reactionary movement; and when they found that Abd el

Aziz could not be made to act consistently as Caliph, they deposed him, and thus opened a way for the true hero of their idea, the present Sultan, Abd el Hamid.

The advent of this latest scion of the house of Othman to the spiritual succession of the Prophet, though a godsend in appearance to religious Moslems, cannot but be regarded by all who wish Islam well as a very great misfortune. It is almost certain that if Abd el Mejid and Abd el Aziz had been succeeded by another of those senseless monarchs who have so often filled the Imperial throne, the Ottoman Caliphate would already have been a thing of the past, at least as regards the larger and more intelligent part of Islam. In the collapse of its physical power in 1879, the official camarilla of Constantinople would have been unable to control the movement of revolt against the spiritual and temporal sovereignty of the Sultan, and something would have taken its place offering a more possible foundation for true religious reform. Arabia would in all probability have by this time asserted its independence, and under a new Caliphate of the Koreysh would have been attracting the sympathies and the adhesion of the Eastern world. There might have been schisms and religious convulsions, but at least there would have been life; and what Islam requires is to live. But unfortunately Abd el Hamid was neither a mere voluptuary nor an imbecile, and catching, by an instinct which one cannot but admire, the one rope of safety which remained for him and his house, he placed himself at the head of the extreme reactionary party of Islam, and thus put back for a while the hour of fate.

It is difficult to gain accurate information as to Abd el Hamid's character and religious opinions, but I believe it may be safely asserted that he represents in these latter the extremest Hanefite views. In youth he was, for a prince, a serious man, showing a taste for learning, especially for geography and history; and though not an *alem* he has some knowledge of his religion. It may therefore be taken for granted that he is sincere in his belief of his own spiritual position—it is easy to be sincere where one's interest lies in believing; and I have it from one who saw him at the time that on the day soon after his accession, when, according to the custom already mentioned, he received the sword at the mosque of Ayub, he astonished his courtiers with the sudden change in his demeanour. All the afternoon of that day he talked to them of his spiritual rank in language which for centuries had not been heard in the precincts of the Seraglio. It is certain, too, that his first act, when delivered from the pressure of the Russian invasion, was to organize afresh the propagandism already begun, and to send out new missionaries to India and the Barbary States to preach the doctrine of his own Caliphal authority to the Moslems *in partibus infidelium*. His language, too, to strangers from external Islam was from the first that of a spiritual rather than a temporal prince, and with the European Ambassadors he has used this position consistently and most effectually.

It is no mean proof of Abd el Hamid's ability that he should have invented the Mussulman *non possumus* with which he has disconcerted our diplomacy. In private life he is said to be regular at his prayers, though it is also said that he conforms to the custom of Turkish Sultans in avoiding legal marriage. He is at the same time a liberal patron of dervishes, workers of miracles, and holy men. These he is at pains to seek out and receive honourably. In his administration he conforms, wherever he is himself the actor, strictly to the Sheriat, and on doubtful points consults always the mufti or Sheykh el Islam. He has shown no inconsiderable firmness in resisting European demands when they contravened the canon law.[13]

For all these reasons it will be readily understood that Abd el Hamid has gained not only the support of his own Turkish Ulema, but the sympathy of a very considerable section of opinion outside his dominions. From a traitor to the cause of religion the Ottoman Sultan has come to be looked upon, east and west, as once more its champion; and with the old-fashioned reactionary school Abd el Hamid is fast growing into a hero. A year ago, when I was at Jeddah, this was not yet the case, but it would seem to be so now. Then even the people of his own party spoke of him doubtfully, and he certainly excited no enthusiasm among them. They did not understand him, and thought that he was playing a part. He was said to be of Armenian parentage (on his mother's side) and his sincerity as a Moslem was suspected. It seemed impossible one born in Abd el Mejid's Seraglio should be a serious man. Besides, he had not yet shown his strength, and to be strong is to be a hero everywhere.

But within the last eight months, events have marched rapidly. Abd el Hamid has played his cards successfully in Greece, in Albania, and with the Kurds. He has not been afraid of England and has shown a bold front against infidel reforms. He has had the courage under the eyes of Europe to arrest their *protege*, Midhat, and to try him for murder. Lastly, the French have played into his hands in Tunis, and he has thus gained a footing of sympathy with the Mussulmans of North Africa, a population which has for centuries opposed his claims. Twenty years ago it would have been absolutely impossible for an Ottoman Sultan to awaken any loyal feeling in any Arab breast. Tunis then specially boasted her independence of the Porte, and all but the Hanefite rulers of the sea-coast towns of Africa would have scouted the idea of fighting for the Turk. Now the Malekites themselves, the puritans of Kerwan, are moving at Abd el Hamid's nod. He would seem, too, to be stirring with some success in Egypt, and Indian Mussulmans are praying for him publicly in their mosques. Everywhere the reactionary party is standing to its arms, and is beginning to recognize a leader in this supple Armenian Khalifeh, who is defying Europe, and seems willing, if necessary, to lead them one day on a Jehad.

With all this, however, it must not be supposed that Orthodox Islam is by any means yet won back to Constantinople. Turkey, I have shown, and the Hanefite school, are far from being the whole of the Mohammedan world; and side by side with the fanatical obduracy of the Ottoman State party and the still fiercer puritanism of the Melkites there exists an intelligent and hopeful party favourable to religious reform. Shafite Egypt is its

stronghold, but it is powerful too in Arabia and further
East. With it a first article of faith is that the House of
Othman has been and is the curse of Islam, and that its
end is at hand.

In spite of Abd el Hamid's pious appeals to the Sheriat
they look upon him as one who troubleth Islam. He is
the representative of the party most bitterly opposed to all
of good. They know that as long as there is an Ottoman
Caliph, whether his name be Abd el Aziz or Abd el Hamid,
moral progress is impossible, that the ijtahad cannot be re-
opened, and that no such reformation of doctrine and
practice can be attempted as would alone enable their
faith to cope with modern infidelity. They see moreover
that, notwithstanding his affected legality, Abd el Hamid's
rule is neither juster nor more in accordance with the
Mussulman law than that of his predecessors. The same
vices of administration are found in it, and the same
recklessness for his Mussulman subjects' welfare. Of all the
lands of Islam his own are probably those where Abd el
Hamid has now the most scanty following. Constantinople
is after all his weak point, for the Young Turkish school is
far from dead, the vicissitudes of life and death follow
each other closely on the Bosphorus, and the liberal party
can better afford than the reactionary to wait. The death
or fall of Abd el Hamid, whenever it may happen, would
immediately decide a movement counter to the Ottoman
Caliphate.

NOTES

[10] I do not vouch for the entire accuracy of these dates. Turkish historians place Selim's death in 926 A.H., which should correspond with our 1520. It would seem doubtful too whether Selim himself took any higher title with regard to the Holy Places than Khadam el Harameyn, Servant of the two shrines, though his successors are certainly called Hami. It was not till five years after Selim's death that Mecca acknowledged the Ottoman Caliphate.

[11] The original diary of Lascaris, Napoleon's agent with the Arabs, has, I understand, within the last two years been discovered at Aleppo and purchased by the French Government. Its publication, whenever that may be decided on, will, if I am not quite mistaken, throw new and important light on Napoleon's Egyptian career.

[12] The *Jawaib* was first started about the year 1860.

[13] In the recent trial of the murderers of Abd el Aziz, Abd el Hamid has departed from his usual adherence to the Sheriat. It is a lapsus which may one day be taken hold of against him, should the Ulema need to depose him. He is said to have yielded to the advice of an European confidant who directs the details of his diplomacy with Europe.

III

The True Metropolis— Mecca

In the last chapter the position of the Ottoman Sultans towards the mass of Orthodox Islam was sketched, and the foundations were shown on which their tenure of the Caliphal title rested. These I explained to be neither very ancient nor very securely laid in the faith and affections of the faithful; and, though at the present moment a certain reaction in favour of Constantinople had set in, it was due to accidental circumstances, which are unlikely to become permanent, and was very far indeed from being universal. It may be as well to recapitulate the position.

The Sunite or Orthodox Mohammedan world holds it as a dogma of faith that there must be a Khalifeh, the ex-officio head of their religious polity, and the successor of their prophet. In temporal matters, whoever holds this office is theoretically king of all Islam; and in spiritual matters he is their supreme religious authority. But, practically, the Caliph's temporal jurisdiction has for many centuries been limited to such lands as he could hold by arms; while in spiritual matters he has exercised no direct authority whatever. Nevertheless, he represents to Mussulmans something of which they are in need, and which they are bound to respect; and it cannot be doubted that in proper hands, and at the proper moment, the Caliphate might once more become an instrument for good or evil of almost universal power in Islam. Even now, were there to be an apprehension of general and overwhelming danger for religion, it is to the Caliph that the faithful would look to defend their interests; and, as we have seen, a moderate show of piety and respect for the sacred law has been sufficient, in spite of a violent political opposition, to secure for the actual holder of the title a degree of sympathy which no other Mussulman prince could at any cost of good government have obtained.

On the other hand, it has been shown that the loyalty, such as there is, which Abd el Hamid inspires is due to him solely as incumbent of the Caliphal office, and not as the representative of any race or dynasty. The House of Othman, as such, represents nothing sacred to Mussulmans; and the Turkish race is very far from being respected in Islam. The present Caliphal house is unconnected in blood with the old traditional line of "successors;" and even with the Turks themselves inspires little modern reverence. Moreover, the actual incumbent of the office is thought to be not even a true Ottoman, being the offspring of the Seraglio rather than of known parents; Abd el Hamid's sole title to spiritual consideration is his official name. This he has had the sense to set prominently forward. Reduced to a syllogism, Mussulman loyalty may be read thus: There must be a Caliph, and the Caliphate deserves respect; there is no other Caliph but Abd el Hamid; ergo, Abd el Hamid deserves respect.

It has been pointed out, however, that, if the Sultan's recent revival of spiritual pretensions is his present . strength, it may also in the immediate future become his weakness. The challenge which the Constantinople school of Hanefism threw down ten years ago to the world has been taken up; and all the learned world now knows the frailty of the House of Othman's spiritual position. The true history of the Caliphate has been published and set side by side with that Turkish history which the ignorance of a previous generation had come to confound with it. At the present day nobody with any instruction doubts that Abd el Hamid and his house might be legally displaced by the first successful rival, and that the only right of Constantinople to lead Islam is the right of the sword. As long as the Ottoman Empire is maintained and no counter Caliph appears, so long will the Sultan be the acknowledged head of religion; but not a day longer. The Caliphate, for one alien as Abd el Hamid is to the Koreysh, must be constantly maintained in arms, and on the first substantial success of a new pretender his present following would fall off from him without compunction, transferring to this last their loyalty on precisely the same ground on which Abd el Hamid now receives it. Abd el Hamid would then be legitimately deposed and disappear, for it is unlikely that he would find any such protector in his adversity as the legitimate Caliphs found in theirs six hundred years ago. So fully is this state of things recognized by the Ulema, that I found the opinion last year to be nearly universal that Abd el Hamid was destined to be the last Caliph of the House of Othman.

It becomes, therefore, a question of extreme interest to consider who among Mussulman princes could, with any chance of being generally accepted by orthodox Islam, put in a claim to replace the Ottoman dynasty as Caliph when the day of its doom shall have been reached. It is a question which ought certainly to interest Englishmen, for on its solution the whole problem of Mussulman loyalty or revolt in India most probably depends, and though it would certainly be unwise, at the present moment, for an English Government to obtrude itself violently in a religious quarrel not yet ripe, much might be done in a perfectly legitimate way to influence the natural course of events and direct it to a channel favourable to British interests.

Is there then in Islam, east, or west, or south, a man of sufficient eminence and courage to proclaim himself Caliph, in the event of Abd el Hamid's political collapse or death? What would be his line of action to secure Mahommedan acceptance? Where should he fix his capital, and on what arms should he rely? Whose flag should he display? Above all—for this is the question that interests us most—could such a change of rulers affect favourably the future thought and life of Islam, and lead to an honest Moslem reformation? These questions, which are being cautiously asked of each other by thoughtful Mussulmans in every corner of the east, I now propose to consider and, as far as it is in my power, to answer.

I have said that Islam is already well prepared for change. Whatever Europeans may think of a future for the Ottoman Empire, Mussulmans are profoundly convinced that on its present basis it will not long survive. Even in Turkey, the thought of its political regeneration as an European Empire has been at last abandoned, and no one now contemplates more than a few years further tenure of the Bosphorus. Twenty years ago it was not so, nor perhaps five, but to-day all are resigned to this.

Ancient prophecy and modern superstition alike point to a return of the Crescent into Asia as an event at hand, and to the doom of the Turks as a race which has corrupted Islam. A well-known prediction to this effect, which has for ages exercised its influence on the vulgar and even the learned Mohammedan mind, gives the year 1883 of our era as the term within which these things are to be accomplished, and places the scene of the last struggle in Northern Syria, at Homs, on the Orontes. Islam is then finally to retire from the north, and the Turkish rule to cease. Such prophecies often work their own fulfilment, and the feeling of a coming catastrophe is so deeply rooted and so universal that I question whether the proclamation of a Jehad by the Sultan would now induce a thousand Moslems to fight voluntarily against the Cross in Europe.

The Sultan himself and the old Turkish party which supports him, while clinging obstinately in appearance to all their ground, really have their eyes turned elsewhere than on Adrianople and Salonica and the city of the Roman Emperors. It is unlikely that a new advance of the Christian Powers from the Balkan would meet again with more than formal opposition; and Constantinople itself, unsupported by European aid, would be abandoned without a blow, or with only such show of resistance as the Sheriat requires for a cession of territory.[14] The Sultan would, in such an event, pass into Asia, and I have been credibly informed that his own plan is to make not Broussa, but Bagdad or Damascus his capital. This he considers would be more in conformity with Caliphal traditions, and the Caliphate would gain strength by a return to its old centres. Damascus is surnamed by theologians *Bab el Kaaba*, Gate of the Caaba; and there or at Bagdad, the traditional city of the Caliphs, he would build up once more a purely theocratic empire.

Such, they say, is his thought; and such doubtless would be the empire of the future that Mussulmans would choose. Only it is improbable that it would continue to be in any sense Ottoman, or that Abd el Hamid would have the opportunity of himself establishing it. The loss of Constantinople would be a blow to his prestige he could not well recover from, and no new empire ever yet was founded on defeat. What is far more likely to happen is that, in such an event, Abd el Hamid and his house would disappear, and an entirely new order of Caliphal succession take their place. Even without supposing any such convulsion to the empire as a loss of the Bosphorus, his reign will hardly be a long one. The Ulema of Constantinople are by no means all on his side, and the party of "Young Turkey," cowed for the moment by the terrorism which there prevails, is his bitter enemy, and will not let him rest. It will infallibly on the next danger from Europe, show its head again and take its revenge.

It is said to be the programme of this party, when it next comes to power, to separate the spiritual functions of the Caliphate from those of the head of the State, copying, in so far, the modern practice of Europe towards the Papacy. I suppose that it would be attempted to restore that state of things, which as we have already seen, existed at Cairo in the fourteenth and fifteenth centuries; and it is just conceivable that, as far as Turkey itself was concerned, such an arrangement might, for a time, succeed. There would then be two powers at Constantinople, a Maire du Palais who would reign, and a Caliph who would be head of religion;—a separation of offices which would certainly facilitate the sort of reform that Midhat and his friends desire. But to the world at large the event would only signify that Constantinople had formally abdicated her claim to leadership, and Islam would never acknowledge as Caliph the mere puppet of an irreligious clique of officials, because he happened to be a member of the Beni Othman. His political power is the only thing that reconciles Islam with an Ottoman Caliph, and without sovereignty he would be discarded. In whatever way, therefore, that we look at it, there seems justification in probability for the conviction already cited that after Abd el Hamid a new order of Caliphal succession will be seen.

It seems to be an universal opinion at the present day among those who think at all upon the matter, that whatever change may be impending for Islam, it will be in the direction of concentration rather than of extension. All parties see that the day of outside conquest is at an end, and that the utmost that Islam can look forward to politically is the maintenance of its present positions, and as an extreme possibility the emancipation of its lost provinces in India and North Africa from Christian rule. There is, therefore, a conviction that the removal of the seat of supreme authority, when made, will be towards the centre, not to any new extremity of Islam. Constantinople, even if all Islam were combined for its defence, is felt to be too near the infidel frontier to be safe, and cosmopolitan city as it has become, it is by many looked upon itself as infidel. A position further removed from danger and more purely Mohammedan is the necessity of the day; and it can hardly be doubted that, when the time comes, the possession of some such vantage ground will be recognized as a first qualification with whoever shall assume the leadership of Islam.

We have seen that Abd el Hamid dreams of Damascus or Bagdad. But others dream of Cairo as the new seat of the Caliphate; and to the majority of far-sighted Mussulmans it is rapidly becoming apparent that the retreat, once begun, must be conducted further still, and that the only true resting-place for theocracy is in Arabia, its birthplace and the fountain head of its inspiration. There, alone in the world, all the conditions for the independent exercise of religious sovereignty are to be found. In Arabia there are neither Christians nor Jews nor infidels of any sort for Islam to count with, nor is it so rich a possession that it should ever excite the cupidity of the Western Powers. A Caliph there need fear no admonition from frank ambassadors in virtue of any capitulations; he would be free to act as the Successor of the Apostle should, and would breathe the pure air of an unadulterated Islam. A return, therefore, to Medina or Mecca is the probable future of the Caliphate.

The importance of Arabia has of late years been fully recognized both at Constantinople and elsewhere. It has been the sustained policy of Abd el Hamid at all cost and by whatsoever means to maintain his influence there; and he knows that without it his spiritual pretensions could have no secure foundations. Arabia, he perceives, is the main point of the Caliphal problem; and whether or not the future holder of the office reside in Hejaz, it is certain that by its tenure alone the Mohammedan world will judge of his right to be their leader. It will, therefore, before we go further, be interesting to examine the relations existing in the past and present between Mecca and the Caliphate, and to ascertain the position now held by Abd el Hamid in Arabia. On this point I believe that I can offer information which will be both valuable and new.

The political constitution of the Moslem Holy Land is one of the most anomalous in the world. Like every district of Arabia proper, Hejaz has a town and a nomad population, but almost no intermediate agricultural class. The townsmen I have already described—a multitude of mixed origin, descended from such pilgrims as from every quarter of the globe have visited the Holy Places, and have remained to marry and die in them. The Nomads, on the contrary, are a pure race of a peculiarly noble type, and unchanged in any essential feature of their life from what they were in the days of Mohammed. They are warlike, unquiet, Bedouins, camel-riders (for they have no horses), and armed with matchlocks; and they are proud of their independence, and tenacious of their rights. No serious attempt has ever been made, except by Mehemet Ali, to subdue them, and none at all has succeeded. Unlike the generality of Peninsular Bedouins, however, they are professed Sunite Mohammedans, if not of a very pious type; and they acknowledge as their chief the head of their most noble tribe, the Grand Sherif of the Koreysh, who is also Prince of Mecca.

The Koreysh is still a distinct nomadic tribe, inhabiting the immediate neighbourhood of Mecca; not numerous, but not in decay. They are divided into several sections, each governed by its Sheykh, the chief of which, the Abadleh, has for several centuries supplied the reigning family of Hejaz. This last traces its descent from Ali ibn Abutaleb, the fourth Caliph, through his son Hassan, and through Ali's wife, Fatmeh, from Mohammed himself. It is probably the oldest authentic male descent in the world, and certainly the most sacred. All the members of this Abadleh family enjoy the title of Sherif, the head of it only being distinguished as the Sherif el Kebir, the Great or Grand Sherif. The rest of the Koreysh, not being descended from Fatmeh, do not receive the title. All alike wear the Bedouin dress of abba and kefiyeh, even the Prince himself, standing in this strikingly in contrast with the Hejazi citizens, who affect the turban and gombaz.

The district of Medina is occupied by the Harb Bedouins, a larger and more powerful tribe than the Koreysh, who also recognize the Sherif, but their allegiance is precarious; while to the east and south of Mecca the Ateybeh and Assir, more powerful still, are wholly independent. It has always been a difficult matter to keep these unruly elements at peace with each other and with the citizens, nor could the Sherif hope to effect it were he not himself of Bedouin and noble blood.

The early history of the Sherifate is exceedingly obscure. When the Caliphs definitely abandoned Medina as their capital in the fortieth year of Islam (A.D. 662), they for a time left deputies of the Sherifal family behind them to govern in their name, and, as long as the Ommiad and Abbaside dynasties continued at Damascus and Bagdad, their sovereignty was acknowledged in Hejaz. But on the destruction of the Arabian Caliphate in 1259, the Sherifal family seems to have set itself up independently, relying only on the casual help of the Egyptian Sultans and the Imams of Sana to protect them against the Bedouins of Nejd and Assir, now hardly any longer, even in name, Mohammedans. The Egyptian Sultan, however, was the titular protector of the Holy Places, and it was he who transmitted the Surrah, or religious contributions made by the Faithful, and provided escort for the yearly pilgrimage made to the shrines. Thus we read of Kaid Beg having rebuilt the Mosque of Medina in 1476, and having sent a yearly subsidy of 7500 ardebs of corn for the townspeople. Other princes, however, contributed their offerings too, and received titles of honour connected with the Holy Land, the Shahs of Persia, the Moguls, and the Ottomans. The first connection of the latter with Mecca that I can find was in 1413, when the Padishah Mohammed Khan I., having sent a surrah, or bag of gold, to the Sherif to be distributed in alms, received from him the title of Khaddam el Harameyn, servant of the two shrines; and the gift being continued annually by the Ottoman Padishahs may very likely have paved the way to their recognition later as Caliphs.

It would seem singular at first sight that the Sherifs, being themselves of the sacred family whose special inheritance the Caliphate was, should ever thus have recognized a stranger as its legal heir. But the political weakness of the Meccan Government in the sixteenth century must be taken into account as the all-sufficient reason. The Grand Sherif could hardly have stood alone as an independent sovereign, for he was continually menaced on the one side by the dissenting Omani, and on the other by the unbelieving tribes of Nejd, against whom his frontier was defenceless. He could not, with his own resources, protect the pilgrim routes from plunder—and on the pilgrimage all the prosperity of Hejaz depended. It therefore was a necessity with the Meccans to have a protector of some sort; and Sultan Kansaw having fallen, they accepted Sultan Selim.

The Ottoman Sultans then became protectors of the Holy Places, and were acknowledged Caliphs without any appeal to arms at Mecca and Medina. Their weapons were, in fact, the gold and silver pieces with which they subsidized the Sherifs. Sultan Selim at once, on being acknowledged, ordered an additional annuity of 5000 ardebs to be paid to Mecca, and he and his immediate successors carried out at their own expense such public works as the shrines required in the way of repairs or improvements. Subsequently the seaport of Jeddah, formerly occupied by the Egyptians, received a Turkish contingent, but the interior of Hejaz was never subjugated, nor was any tax at any time levied. Only once a year an Ottoman army appeared before the walls of Medina, conducting the pilgrims from Damascus and convoying the surrah. The state of things at Mecca in the last century has been clearly sketched by Niebuhr. The Sherifs were in reality independent princes, but they "gratified the vanity of the Grand Signior" by calling him their suzerain, he on his side occasionally exercising the right of power by deposing the reigning Sherif and appointing another of the same family. No kind of administration had then been attempted by the Turks in Hejaz.

Mehemet Ali's occupation of Hejaz in 1812 first brought foreign troops inland. He established himself at Taif, the summer residence of the Meccans; deposed the Grand Sherif Ghaleb, and appointed in his stead another member of the Sherifal family; declaring the Sultan sovereign of the country—acts which the Meccans acquiesced in through dread of the Wahhabis, from whom Mehemet Ali promised to deliver them. The Egyptian and Turkish Governments have thus, during the present century, exercised some of the functions of sovereignty in Hejaz.

At the present moment Sultan Abd el Hamid's position in the country is this. His troops occupy Jeddah and Yembo, the two seaports, and the towns of Medina and Taif in the interior. He is acknowledged by the Sherifs as sovereign, except in Mecca; and he appoints to all the principal offices of State, including the supreme office of the Grand Sherifate itself. He is represented by a Pasha who resides alternately at Jeddah and Taif according to the season, but who has not the right of entering Mecca without the Grand Sherif's leave, or of sending troops there. The total garrison of the Turks in Hejaz last winter was from 8000 to 10,000 men, of whom 4000 only were regulars (Nizams), and efficient. While I was at Jeddah, the Medina garrison of 2000 regulars, having been long unpaid and unrationed, was said to be living on public charity. On the other hand the Hejazi Bedouins do not acknowledge any sovereignty but that of the Sherif, nor could the Sultan pretend to keep order outside the towns except through the Sherif's interposition. The Sultan levies no tax in the interior or impost of any kind, and the sole revenue he receives in Hejaz comes from Customs duties of Jeddah and Yembo, which may amount to L40,000.

In return for this he also is bound to transmit every year at the time of the pilgrimage sums of money collected by him from the revenues of the Wakaf within his dominions, lands settled by pious persons on the Sherifal family. These are said to amount to nearly half a million sterling, and are distributed amongst all the principal personages of Hejaz. The transmission of the Wakaf income, in which the Sultan constitutes himself, so to say, the Sherif's agent, is in fact the real bond which unites Hejaz with the Caliphate, and its distribution gives the Sultan patronage, and with it power in the country. The bond, however, is one of interest only. The Sherifs, proud of their sacred ancestry, look upon the Turkish Caliphs as barbarians and impostors, while the Sultans find the Hejaz a heavy charge upon their revenue. Either hates and despises the other, the patron and the patronized; and, save that their union is a necessity, it would long ago have, by mutual consent, been dissolved. The Sherif depends upon the Sultan because he needs a protector, and needs his Wakaf. The Sultan depends upon the Sherif, because recognition by Hejaz as the protector is a chief title to his Caliphate. Mecca, in fact, is a necessity to Islam even more than a Caliph; and whoever is sovereign there is naturally sovereign of the Mussulman world.

Outside Hejaz the Sultan holds what he holds of Arabia merely by force. I have described already the growing power of Ibn Rashid, the Prince of Nejd; and since that time, two years ago, he has sensibly extended and confirmed his influence there. He has now brought into his alliance all the important tribes of northern Arabia, including the powerful Ateybeh, who, a few months ago, were threatening Mecca; and in Hejaz his name is already as potent as the Sultan's. He offered, while I was at Jeddah, to undertake the whole convoy of the Damascus pilgrimage with his own troops, as already he convoys that from Persia; while I have quite recent information of a campaign against his own rivals, the Ibn Saouds, which he has just brought to a successful conclusion. In Yemen, the other neighbour of the Meccans, 20,000 Turkish troops are required to garrison the few towns the Sultan calls his own, and were it not for the facility given him by the possession of the sea-coast, these could not long hope to hold their ground. Every day I am expecting news from there of a revolt, and the first sign of weakness at Constantinople will certainly precipitate a war of independence in that part of Arabia.

We may expect, therefore, in the event of such a break-up as I have suggested to be likely of the Ottoman power—either through loss of territory or by the growing impoverishment of the empire, which needs must, in a few decades, end in atrophy—to see among Mussulman princes a competition for the right of protecting the Holy Places, and with it of inheriting the Caliphal title. The Sultan reduced to Asia Minor, even if he retain Armenia and Kurdistan (which is extremely improbable), would be quite unable to afford himself the expensive luxury of holding his Arabian conquests and buying the patronage of Mecca. He would be unable any longer to overawe the Red Sea, or secure the pilgrim routes. The Princes of Nejd would certainly not tolerate the presence of Turkish soldiers at Medina, and the Sherifs of Mecca would have to make terms with them and with the restored Imams of Yemen till such time as they should find a new protector elsewhere. Above all, the half million of Wakaf income would no longer be forthcoming, and a Turkish Emir el Haj arriving empty-handed at Mecca would bring his master to a climax of derision. Hejaz then would infallibly look out for a new potentate whom she could dignify with the title of Hami el Harameyn and Emir el Mumenin; and if there were none forthcoming would herself proclaim a Caliphate. Let us look, therefore, at the lands of Islam to see in which of them a competent Prince of the Faithful is likely to appear.

It is possible, though to European eyes it will seem far from probable, that out of the ferment which we are now witnessing in the Barbary States, some leader of real power and religious distinction may arise who shall possess the talent of banding together into an instrument of power the immense but scattered forces of Islam in Northern Africa, and after achieving some signal success against the new French policy, establish himself in Tripoli or Tunis in independent sovereignty. Were such another man as Abd el Kader to arise, a saint, a preacher, and a soldier, indifferent to the petty aims of local power and gifted with military genius, true piety, and an eloquent tongue, I believe at the present day he might achieve at least a partial success.

The French army is weak in discipline and confidence compared to what it was in Abd el Kader's day, and it has a far more difficult frontier to defend; while the Government at home is but half resolute, and the Arabs command much floating sympathy in Europe and elsewhere. I do not say the thing is likely, but it is conceivable; and Africa contains the elements of a possible new sovereignty for some Mussulman prince which might eventually lead him on the road to Mecca. It is undoubted that with the prestige of success against a Christian Power, and backed by the vast populations of Soudan and the fierce military fervour of the Malekite Arabs, an Abd el Kader or an Abd-el-Wahhab would attract the sympathy of Islam, and might aspire to its highest dignity. But enormous postulates must be granted before we can look on any one now known to fame in Africa as a probable candidate for the future Caliphate.

The present leaders of the Arabs are but local heroes, and as yet they have achieved nothing which can command respect. In Tripoli there is indeed a saint of very high pretensions, one known as the Sheykh Es Snusi, who has a large religious following, and who has promised to come forward shortly as the Mohdy or guide expected by a large section of the Sunite as well as the Shiite Mussulmans. Next year he will attain the age of forty (the legal age of a prophet), and he may be expected to take a prominent part in any general movement that may then be on foot. But as yet we know nothing of him but his name and the fact of his sanctity, which is of Wahhabite type. Moreover, even supposing all that may be supposed of a possible success, there yet lies Egypt and the Suez Canal between the Barbary State and Mecca, so that I think we may be justified in these days of steam fleets and electric cables and European concerts, if we treat North Western

Africa as out of probable calculations in considering the future of the Caliphate. It is remarkable that the Sultan of Morocco has taken as yet no apparent part in the religious movement of modern Barbary.

The Mussulman princes of India hold a very similar position. Opposed as they soon may be, indeed must be if the unintelligent English policy of the last twenty years be persevered in, to an European Government in arms, they will have the chance of making themselves a leading position in the eyes of Islam; and should a Mohammedan empire arise once more at Delhi or Hyderabad, India would certainly become *par excellence* the Dar el Islam. It would then be by far the richest and most populous of Mohammedan states, and able to outbid any other with the surrah it could send to Mecca.

The Wakaf property in India at the present day is supposed to be as valuable as that in the Ottoman empire, and it would then become a source of patronage with the Government, instead of being privately remitted as now. If money alone could buy the Caliphate, a successful leader of revolt against the English in India might dictate his terms to Islam. But again the insuperable obstacle intervenes of distance and the sea. Mussulman India could never give that protection to Mecca that Islam needs, and could not assert its sovereignty anywhere but at home, in arms. Even this is assuming, as in the case of Barbary, an enormous postulate—success.

Neither India, then, nor Western Africa can reasonably be expected to supply that substitute for the House of

Othman which we need. A more apparent and in the opinion of some a likely candidate for the Caliphate succession may be looked for in the Viceregal family of Egypt. Mohammed Towfik, if he were a man of genius like his grandfather, or if, honest man as he is, he plays his cards with success, might in a few years become an important rival at Mecca to the Sultan. To say nothing of its traditional connection with the Caliphate, Egypt has the more modern recollection of Mehemet Ali to urge upon the Hejazi in its favour as the protecting State of Islam.

Mehemet Ali's name and that of his successor Ibrahim Pasha, if not precisely popular, are at least respected at Mecca; and the latter possesses a great title to Sunite gratitude in having destroyed the Wahhabite empire in 1818. I have mentioned Mehemet Ali's ambition; and a similar ambition would seem to have occurred to Ismail, the late Khedive. He, in the plenitude of his financial power, is stated to have expended large sums of money in subsidising the Sherifs with a view to possible contingencies at Constantinople. But unfortunately for him the opening of the Suez Canal, on which he had counted for securing him the support of Europe, proved the precise instrument of ruin for his scheme.

The Porte in 1871, scenting danger to its own Caliphal pretensions from this quarter, occupied the Red Sea in force, reinforced its garrisons in Jeddah and Yembo, advanced to Taif, and threw a large army into Yemen. This was alone made possible by the Canal, and Ismail to his chagrin found himself "hoist with his own petard." Mohammed Towfik, therefore, would have some excuse in family tradition if he indulged occasionally in dreams of a similar nature. His connection with Mecca is at the present day second only to that of Constantinople; the Egyptian Khedivieh line of steamers ply constantly between Suez and Jeddah; and the Haj the Khedive sends to Mecca, including as it does most of the Mogrebbin pilgrims, is more numerous than the Sultan's. He maintains intimate relations with one at least of the great Sherifal families, and sends a Mahmal yearly with an important surrah to Medina. Mohammed Towfik also has the deserved reputation of being a sincere Mussulman and an honest man, and it is certain that a large section of true liberal opinion looks to him as the worthiest supporter of its views. With all this I doubt if he be big enough a man to aspire as yet with success to Abd el Hamid's succession.

The present Viceroy's financial position, though we may hope sounder in its base, is not so immediately powerful as his father's; and much ready money will be required by an aspirant to the Caliphate. His fighting power, too, is small, and he would have to proclaim himself in arms. Moreover—and this I fear will remain an insuperable difficulty—he is hampered with the control of Europe. Islam would hardly obey another Caliph who was himself obedient to Christendom; and the same causes which have ruined the House of Othman, would also ruin him. A Caliph, as things stand, cannot legally govern, except by the old canon law of the Sheriat, and though a lapsus from strict observance may be tolerated in an ordinary prince, or even in a well established Caliph, a new Caliph putting forward a new claim would be more strictly bound. How could Mohammed Towfik's necessity to Islam be reconciled to his necessity to Europe? Between the two stools he hardly could avert a fall.[15]

Unless, then, some unexpected religious hero should appear in Eastern Asia, of which as yet there is no sign, we are driven to Arabia for a solution of the difficulty where to establish a Mussulman theocracy, and to the Sherifal family of Mecca itself for a new dynasty.

The family of the Sherifs has this vast advantage over any other possible competitor to the supreme title of Islam, that it is of the acknowledged blood of that tribe of Koreysh which Mohammed himself designated as his heirs. Amongst many other passages of authority which bear upon the rights of the Koreysh the following seem to me the most explicit and the best worth quoting: "The prophet", says a tradition of Omm Hani, daughter of Abutaleb, "exalted the Koreysh by conferring on them seven prerogatives: the first, the *Nebbuwat* (the fact that they had given birth to a prophet); the second, the *Khalafat* (the succession); the third, the *Hejabat* (the guardianship of the Kaaba); the fourth, the *Sikayat* (the right of supplying water to the Haj); the fifth, the *Refadat* (the right of entertaining the Haj); the sixth, the *Nedwat* (the right of counsel, government); and the seventh, the *Lewa* (possession of the banner, with the right of proclaiming war)." The prophet also, according to another tradition, said, "As long as there remains one man of the Koreysh, so long shall that man be my successor;" and as to the Arab race, "If the Arab race falls Islam shall fall." All the world knows these things, and to the popular mind, especially, the Sherif is already far more truly the representative of spiritual rank than any Sultan or Caliph is.

The vast populations of Southern and Eastern Asia send out their pilgrims, not to Constantinople but to Mecca, and it is the Sherif whom they find there supreme. The Turkish Government in Hejaz holds a comparatively insignificant position, and the Sultan's representative at Jeddah is hardly more than servant to the Prince of Mecca. It is he who is the descendant of their prophet, not the other, and though the learned may make distinctions in favour of the Caliph the Haj only hears of the Sherif. Even at Constantinople, by immemorial custom, the Sultan rises to receive members of the sacred family; and at Mecca it is commonly said that should a Sultan make the Haj in person he would be received by the Grand Sherif as an inferior. The Sherifal family, then, is surrounded with a halo of religious prestige which would make their acquisition of the supreme temporal title appear natural to all but the races who have been in subjection to the Ottomans; and were a man of real ability to appear amongst them he would, in the crisis we have foreseen, be sure to find an almost universal following.

That the Ottoman Government is perfectly aware of this is certain. Even in the days of its greatest power it always showed its jealousy and distrust of Mecca, and was careful when any of the Grand Sherifs acquired what was considered dangerous influence, to supplant him by setting up a rival. Its physical power enabled it to do this, and though it could not abolish the office of the Grand Sherifate, it could interfere in the order of succession. Family feuds have, therefore, been at all times fostered by the Turks in Hejaz, and will be, as long as their presence there is tolerated. An excellent example of their system has recently been given in the episode of the late Grand Sherif's death, and the story of it will serve also to show the fear entertained by the present Sultan of this his great spiritual rival. To tell it properly I must go back to the epoch of the Wahhabite invasion of Hejaz in 1808.

At that time, and for the latter half of the previous century, the supreme dignity of the Sherifal House was held by a branch of it known as the Dewy Zeyd (the word *Dewy* is used in Hejaz, as are elsewhere *Beni* or *Ahl*, meaning *people, family, house*), which had replaced in 1750 the Barakat branch, mentioned by Niebuhr as in his day supreme. The actual holder of the title was Ghaleb ibn Mesaad, and he, finding himself unable to contend against the Wahhabis, became himself a Wahhabi. Consequently, when Mehemet Ali appeared at Mecca in 1812, his first act was to depose this Ghaleb, in spite of his protest that he had returned to orthodoxy, and to appoint another member of the Sherifal House in his place.

The Sherif chosen was Yahia ibn Serur, of a rival branch, the Dewy Aoun, and a bitter animosity was, by this means, engendered between the two families of Aoun and Zeyd, which is continued to the present day. Nor, as may be supposed, was this lessened by the subsequent changes rung by the Turkish and Egyptian Governments in their appointments to the office, for, in 1827, we find Abd el Mutalleb, the son of the deposed Wahhabite Ghaleb, reappointed, and in the following year again, Mohammed, the son of Yahia ibn Aoun, an intrigue which brought on a civil war. Then in 1848 a new intrigue reinstated Abd el Mutalleb and the Zeyds; and then, in 1853, these were again deposed for rebellion, and an Aoun was placed in power. From 1853 till 1880 the Aouns retained the Grand Sherifate and were supreme in Hejaz. Coming into power at a time when Liberal ideas were in the ascendant they have consistently been Liberal, and still represent the more humane and progressive party among the Meccans. In the desert, where all are latitudinarian, they are the popular party; and, though themselves beyond a suspicion of unorthodoxy, they have always shown a tolerant spirit towards the Shiahs and other heretics, with whom the Sherifal authority necessarily comes in contact every year at the Haj. They have even maintained friendly terms with the European element at Jeddah, and as long as they remained in power the relations between India and Mecca were of an amicable nature.

Abdallah ibn Aoun, the son of Mohammed, who succeeded his father in 1858, and reigned for nineteen years, was a man of considerable ability, and he is credited with having had views of so advanced a nature as to include the opening of Hejaz to European trade. Nor was his brother, who in 1877 became Grand Sherif, of a less liberal mind. Though of less ability than Abdallah, he is described as eminently humane and virtuous, and it is certain that, with the exception of his hereditary enemies, the Zeyds, he was universally beloved by the Hejazi. So much was this the case that, in the year following the disastrous Russian war, when Constantinople seemed on the point of dissolution, the Arabs began to talk openly of making El Husseyn ibn Aoun Caliph in the Sultan's place. I have not been able to ascertain that El Husseyn himself indulged the ambitious project of his friends, for he was eminently a man of peace, and the Caliphal title would hardly have given him a higher position than he held. But it is certain that his popularity gave umbrage at Constantinople, the more so as Abd el Hamid could not and dared not depose him. El Husseyn, too, became specially obnoxious to the reactionary party, when it resolved at last to quarrel with England, for he and his family persisted in remaining on friendly terms with the British Government on all occasions when the interests of Indian subjects of her Majesty's came in question at the Haj. For this reason, principally, it would seem his death was resolved on to make room for the agent of a new policy.

On the 14th of March, 1880, Jeddah was the scene of a solemn pageant. The Haj was just over, and the seaport of Mecca crowded with pilgrims was waiting for the Grand Sherif, the descendant of the prophet and the representative of the Sacred House of Ali, to give the blessing of his presence to the last departing votaries. Travelling by night from Mecca, El Husseyn and his retinue appeared at dawn outside the city walls, and when it was morning, mounted on a white mare from Nejd, and preceded by his escort of Koreysh Arabs and the Sultan's guard of honour, he rode into the town. The streets of Jeddah are narrow and tortuous, and the way from the gate to the house of Omar Nassif, his agent, where he was accustomed to alight, was thronged with pious folk, who struggled for the privilege of kissing his feet and the hem of his Arab cloak. He had nearly reached the place when an old beggar from the crowd pushed his way forward asking loudly for alms in the name of God. It was an appeal not to be denied, and as the Sherif turned to those near him to order a contribution from the bag kept for such distributions, the old man rose upon him, and drawing a ragged knife (so it was described to me) struck him in the belly. At first, even those who saw the deed hardly knew what had happened, for El Husseyn did not fall or dismount, and without speaking rode on to the house. There he was lifted from his mare and carried to an upper chamber, and in the course of some hours he expired.

Those nearest him, meanwhile, had seized and cudgelled the old man, and some of the escort had taken him to the guard-house. When it became known what had happened, a great cry arose in Jeddah, and old and young, and women and children, and citizens and strangers wept together. I have heard the scene described as one beyond description moving, and the women shrieked and wailed the whole night long. El Husseyn was beloved, and he was taken in the flower of his manhood.

No satisfactory judicial investigation seems to have been made of the deed, though a formal mejlis was held at Mecca whither the assassin was immediately transferred, and on the fourth day he was publicly executed. Who and what he was it is difficult to determine. The Turkish bulletin on the event described him as a Persian fanatic, but no one confessed to having known him, and those who saw and spoke to him while in custody maintain that he was an Afghan and a Sunite. He seems to have given half-a-dozen contradictory accounts of himself; but the general impression remains that he came from Turkey, and was by profession a dervish. He had not come with the Haj, but had been first noticed as a beggar at Mecca ten days before, when he had asked and received an alms of the Sherif, and had since been several times found obtrusively in El Husseyn's path. No one at Jeddah holds the Turkish Governor to have been cognisant of the crime. He was personally on good terms with El Husseyn, and has since been disgraced; but all point to the Stamboul Camarilla and even the Sultan himself as its author. It is known that Abd el Hamid constantly employs dervishes as his spies and private agents, and some who pretend to know best affirm that the old man received his mission directly from the Caliph. I do not affect to decide upon the point, but think the *onus probandi* to lie with those who would deny it.

Assassination of a dangerous rival or of too powerful a chieftain has been the resource time out of mind of the

Ottoman sovereigns, and they can hardly claim indulgence now from public opinion. The Sheykh of the Dervishes is all powerful with his fanatical followers, and he is the Sultan's servant; a word from him would doubtless have secured the services of twenty such devotees. One circumstance points decidedly to Constantinople. It is known in Jeddah that El Husseyn's successor, who had long been resident at Constantinople, sent orders to his agent at Jeddah to prepare for his return as Grand Sherif two months before El Husseyn, who was a young man, died; and that he had, moreover, dispatched most of his baggage in anticipation.

The last words of the old assassin are curious. Having done his deed he seemed quite happy, and neither ate nor drank, but prepared for the next world. A little while before he was executed he related a story. "There was once", he said, "an elephant, a great and noble beast, and to him God sent a gnat, the smallest thing which is. It stung him on the trunk and the elephant died. Allah Kerim: God is merciful."

El Husseyn's successor, the man for whom room was made, and who knew beforehand that it was to be made, was none other than the aged and twice deposed Abd el Mutalleb, the son of the Wahhabite Ghaleb, the fiercest fanatic of the Dewy Zeyd.

I have not room here to describe in detail the effect of this coup de Jarnac on the political aspect of Hejaz. For the moment the reactionary party is in power at Mecca, as it is at Constantinople. Abd el Mutalleb is supported by

Turkish bayonets, and the Aoun family and the Liberals
are suffering persecution at Mecca, while the Sherifal
Court, which had hitherto been most friendly to England,
has become the focus of Indian discontent. Outside the
town all is disorder. It is sufficient for the present if I have
shown that there is in Hejaz an element of spiritual power
already existing side by side with the Sultan, of which
advantage may one day be taken to provide him with a
natural successor. If no new figure should appear on the
political horizon of Islam when the Ottoman empire dies,
sufficiently commanding to attract the allegiance of the
Mussulman world (and of such there is as yet no sign), it
is certainly to the Sherifal family of Mecca that the mass
of Mohammedans would look for a representative of their
supreme headship, and of that Caliphate of which they
stand in need.

The transfer of the seat of spiritual power from
Constantinople to Mecca would be an easy and natural
one, and would hardly disturb the existing ideas of the
vulgar, while it would harmonize with all the traditions of
the learned. Mecca or Medina would, on the extinction
of Constantinople, become almost of necessity the legal
home of the Ahl el Agde, and might easily become the
acknowledged centre of spiritual power. All whom I have
spoken to on the subject agree that the solution would
be an acceptable one to every school of Ulema except
the distinctly Turkish schools. Indeed "Mecca, the seat of
the Caliphate" is, as far as I have had an opportunity of
judging, the cry of the day with Mussulmans; nor is it one

likely to lose strength in the future. Like the cry of "Roma capitale", it seems to exercise a strong influence on the imagination of all to whom it is suggested, and when to that is added "a Caliphate from the Koreysh", the idea is to Arabs at least irresistible. How indeed should it be otherwise when we look back on history?

For my own part, though I do not pretend to determine the course events will take, I consider this notion of a return to Mecca decidedly the most probable of all the contingencies we have reviewed, and the one which gives the best promise of renewed spiritual life for Islam. Politically the Caliph at Mecca would of course be less important than now on the Bosphorus; but religiously he would have a far more assured footing. Every year the pilgrimage from every part of the world would visit him, and instead of representing a mere provincial school of thought, he would then be a true metropolitan for all schools and all nations.

The Arabian element in Islam would certainly support such a nomination, and it must be remembered that Arabia extends from Marocco to Bushire; and so would the Indian and the Malay—indeed every element but the Turkish, which is day by day becoming of less importance. I have even heard it affirmed that a Caliphate of the Koreysh at Mecca would go far towards reconciling the Schismatics, Abadhites, and Shiahs with orthodoxy; and I have reason to believe that it would so affect the liberal three-quarters of Wahhabism. To the Shiahs, especially, a descendant of Ali could not but be acceptable; and to the Arabs of Oman and Yemen a Caliph of the Koreysh would be at least less repugnant than a Caliph of the Beni Othman. There certainly have of late years been symptoms of less bitterness between these schismatics and their old enemies, the Sunites; and such a change in the conditions of the Caliphate might conceivably bring about a full reconciliation of all parties. Mussulmans can no longer afford to fight each other as of old; and I know that a reunion of the sects is already an idea with advanced thinkers. Lastly, the Caliphate would in Arabia be freed from the incubus of Turkish scholasticism and the stigma of Turkish immorality, and would have freer scope for what Islam most of all requires, a moral reformation.

It is surely not beyond the flight of sane imagination to suppose, in the last overwhelming catastrophe of Constantinople, a council of Ulema assembling at Mecca, and according to the legal precedent of ancient days electing a Caliph. The assembly would, without doubt, witness intrigues of princes and quarrels among schoolmen and appeals to fanaticism and accusations of infidelity. Money, too, would certainly play its part there as elsewhere, and perhaps blood might be shed. But any one who remembers the history of the Christian Church in the fifteenth century, and the synods which preceded the Council of Basle, must admit that such accompaniments of intrigue and corruption are no bar to a legal solution of religious difficulties. It was above all else the rivalries of Popes and Anti-popes that precipitated the Catholic Reformation.

NOTES

[14] According to Canon Law the Caliph cannot cede any portion of the lands of Islam except on physical compulsion.

[15] This too was written before the events of September, 1881. These have immensely added to the chance of Cairo's becoming once more the seat of the Caliphate, though not perhaps of Mohammed Towfik's being the Caliph elected.

IV

A Mohammedan Reformation

It is with considerable doubt of my ability to do justice to so very difficult a subject that I now approach the most important point of all in this inquiry, namely, the question on which in reality every other depends: "Is there a possibility of anything like general reform for Islam in her political and moral life?"

It is obvious that, unless we can answer this in the affirmative, none of the changes I have been prefiguring will very much affect her ultimate fortunes—neither the solution of her legal deadlock with the Ottoman Caliphate, nor the transfer of her metropolis to a new centre, nor even the triumph of her arms, if such were possible, in Africa or India. These by themselves could, at best, only delay her decline. They might even precipitate her ruin. Islam, if she relies only on the sword, must in the end perish by it, for her forces, vast as they are, are without physical cohesion, being scattered widely over the surface of three continents and divided by insuperable accidents of seas and deserts; and the enemy she would have to face is intelligent as well as strong, and would not let her rest. Already what is called the "Progress of the World" envelopes her with its ships and its commerce, and, above all, with its printed thought, which she is beginning to read. Nor is it likely in the future to affect her less. Every year as it goes by carries her farther from the possibility of isolation, and forces on her new acquaintances, not only her old foes, the Frank and Muscovite, but the German, the Chinaman, and the American, with all of whom she may have in turn to count. If she would not be strangled by these influences she must use other arms than those of the flesh, and meet the intellectual invasion of her frontiers with a corresponding intelligence. Otherwise she has nothing to look forward to but a gradual decay, spiritual as well as political. Her law must become little by little a dead letter, her Caliphate an obsolete survival, and her creed a mere opinion. Islam as a living and controlling moral force in the world would then gradually cease.

In expressing my conviction that Islam is not thus destined yet awhile to perish I believe that I am running counter to much high authority among my countrymen. I know that it is a received opinion with those best qualified to instruct the public that Islam is in its constitution unamenable to change, and by consequence to progressive life, or even, in the face of hostile elements, to prolonged life at all. Students of the Sheriat have not inaptly compared the Koranic law to a dead man's hand, rigid and cold, and only to be loosened when the hand itself shall have been cut away. It has been asserted that the first rule of Mohammedan thought has been that change was inadmissible, and development of religious practice, either to right or left of the narrow path of mediaeval scholasticism, absolutely precluded. I know this, and I know, too, that a vast array of learned Mohammedan opinion can be cited to prove this to be the case, and that very few of the modern Ulema of any school of divinity would venture openly to impugn its truth. Nor have I forgotten the repeated failure of attempts made in Turkey within the last fifty years to gain religious assent to the various legal innovations decreed by Sultan after Sultan in deference to the will of Europe, nor the fate which has sometimes overtaken those who were the advocates of change. I know, according to all rule written and spoken by the orthodox, that Islam cannot move, and yet in spite of it I answer with some confidence in the fashion of Galileo, "E pur si muove."

The fact is, Islam does move. A vast change has come upon Mohammedan thought since its last legal Mujtahed wrote his last legal opinion; and what was true of orthodox Islam fifty and even twenty years ago is no longer true now. When Urquhart, the first exponent of Mohammedanism to Englishmen, began his writing, the Hanefite teaching of Constantinople had not begun to be questioned, and he was perfectly justified in citing it as the only rule recognized by the mass of the orthodox. No such thing as a liberal religious party then existed anywhere, and those who broke the law in the name of political reform were breakers of the law and nothing more. Every good man was their enemy, and if any spoke of liberty he was understood as meaning licence. It was not even conceived then that the Sheriat might be legally remodelled. Now, however, and especially within the last ten years, a large section of godly and legal-minded men have ranged themselves on the side of liberal opinion, and serious attempts have been made to reconcile a desire of improvement with unabated loyalty to Islam.

A true liberal party has thus been formed, which includes in its ranks not merely political intriguers of the type familiar to Europe in Midhat Pasha, but men of sincere piety, who would introduce moral as well as political reforms into the practice of Mohammedans. These have it in their programme to make the practice of religion more austere while widening its basis, to free the intelligence of believers from scholastic trammels, and at the same time to enforce more strictly the higher moral law of the Koran, which has been so long and so strangely violated. In this they stand in close resemblance to the "Reformers" of Christianity; and some of the circumstances which have given them birth are so analogous to those which Europe encountered in the fifteenth century that it is impossible not to draw in one's own mind a parallel, leading to the conviction that Islam, too, will work out for itself a Reformation.

The two chief agents of religious reform in Europe were the misery of the poor and the general spread of knowledge. It is difficult at this distance of time to conceive how abject was the general state of the European peasantry in the days of Louis XI. of France and Frederick III. of Germany. The constant wars and almost as constant famines, the general insecurity of the conditions of life, the dependence of a vast majority of the poor on capricious patrons, the hideous growth of corruption and licentiousness in the ruling classes, and the impotence of the ruled to obtain justice, above all, the servile acquiescence of religion, which should have protected them, in the political illegalities daily witnessed—all these things, stirring the hearts of men, caused them to cry out against the existing order of Church discipline, and inclined them to Reform. On the other hand, as we all know, the invention of printing had caused men to read and the invention of the New World to travel. Moreover, in the fifteenth century the Ottoman Turks, then an irresistible power, were invading Europe, and a new element of contact with an outside world was created, and a new fear. Christendom certainly at that time was in danger of political annihilation, or fancied itself to be so, and the apprehensions of devout persons in Central Europe were roused to a vivid consciousness of impending evil by the thought that this was perhaps another authorized scourge of God.

I will not strain the parallel further than it will bear, but I would suggest that causes somewhat analogous to these are now at work among the Mussulmans of the still independent states of Islam, and that they are operating somewhat in the same direction. The Mussulman peasantry, especially of the Ottoman Empire, are miserable, and they know that they are so, and they look in vain to their religion to protect them, as in former days, against their rulers. They find that all their world now is corrupt—

that the law is broken daily by those who should enforce the law; that the illegalities of those who ruin them are constantly condoned by a conniving body of the Ulema; that for all practical purposes of justice and mercy religion has abdicated its claim to direct and govern. They have learned, too, by their intercourse with strangers, and in the towns by the newspapers which they now eagerly read, that this has not been always so, and that servitude is not the natural state of man or acquiescence in evil the true position of religion, and they see in all they suffer an outrage inflicted on the better law of Islam. I was much struck by hearing the Egyptian peasantry last year attribute the lighter taxes they were then enjoying to the fact that their new ruler was "a man who feared God."

At the same time the learned classes are shocked and alarmed at the political decline of Islam and the still greater dangers which stare her in the face, and they attribute them to the unchecked wickedness and corruption with which the long rule of Constantinople has pervaded every class of society, even beyond its own territorial borders. They complain now that they have been led astray, and believe that the vengeance of Heaven will overtake them if they do not amend their ways. In all this, I say, there is something of the spirit which once goaded Christians into an examination of the bases on which their belief rested, and of the true nature of the law which tolerated such great corruption.

Nor must we suppose that any part of this dissatisfaction is attributable as yet to a decay of faith, such as we now witness among ourselves. Islam as yet shows hardly a taint of infidelity. The Mussulman of the present day, whatever his rank in life, believes with as absolute a faith as did the Christian of the period just referred to. With the exception of here and there a false convert or, as a very rare case, an Europeanized infidel of the modern type, there is no such thing as a Mohammedan sceptic, that is to say, a Moslem who does not believe in the divine mission of Mohammed. He may neglect every duty of his profession, be guilty of every crime, have broken every law—he may be the worst and the most depraved of men—or, on the other hand, he may have adopted the language and to a certain extent the tone of thought of Europe, and, a thing far more rare, he may be even a scoffer and blasphemer;—still I do not imagine that in his heart he any the less firmly believes that the Koran is the book of truth, or that at the day of judgment he shall be found with those who have escaped Jehannem through their professed acknowledgment of God and of His apostle.

I have heard strange stories in corroboration of this from persons whom I could not doubt, and about persons whom all the world knew. Thus, one who was with Fuad Pasha, the most European of Ottoman diplomatists, in his last days at Nice, assures me that his whole time was spent in a recitation of the Koran, learning it by heart. Another, who was called the Voltaire of Islam, performed his prayers and prostrations with scrupulous regularity whenever he found himself in private; and a third, equally notorious as a sceptic, died of religious mania. All, too, who have mingled much with Mussulmans, must have been struck with the profound resignation with which even thoughtless and irreligious men bear the ills of life, and the fortitude with which they usually meet their end—with the large proportion that they see of men who habitually pray and fast, and who on occasion, at great risk and sacrifice, make the pilgrimage, and with the general absence of profanity, and the fact that an avowal of religion is never proffered apologetically as with us, nor met in any society with derision. These things are, perhaps, not in themselves evidence of belief, for hypocrites have everywhere their reward, but the fact even of hypocrisy proves the general spirit to be one of avowed belief.

The truly devout are doubtless rare, but where we find them it is evident that their belief pervades their lives in as strict a sense as it does devout persons among ourselves. It would probably be difficult to point out in Europe men who in the world—I do not speak of ecclesiastics or persons in religious orders—lead more transparently religious lives than do the pious Moslems of the better class whom one may find in almost any oriental town, or men who more closely follow the ideal which their creed sets before them. To doubt the sincerity and even, in a certain sense, the sanctity of such persons, would be to doubt all religion. In any case it is notorious that the faith of Mecca is still the living belief of a vast number of the human race, the rule of their lives, and the explanation to them of their whole existence. There is no sign as yet that it has ceased to be a living faith.

Neither in considering its future is it easy for a candid English mind to escape the admission that, for all purposes of argument, the Mohammedan creed must be treated as no vain superstition but a true religion, true inasmuch as it is a form of the worship of that one true God in whom Europe, in spite of her modern reason, still believes. As such it is entitled to whatever credit we may give true religions of prolonged vitality; and while admitting the eternal truth of Christianity for ourselves, we may be tempted to believe that in the Arabian mind, if in no other, Islam too will prove eternal.

In its simplest form Islam was but an emphatic renewal of the immemorial creed of the Semites, and as long as a pure Semitic race is left in the world, the revelation of Mecca may be expected to remain a necessary link in their tradition. No modern arguments of science are ever likely to affect the belief of Arabia that God has at sundry times and in sundry places spoken to man by the mouth of his prophets; and among these prophets Mohammed will always be the most conspicuous because the most distinctly national. Also the law of Islam—I am not speaking merely of the Sheriat as we now see it—will always remain their law because it is the codification of their custom, and its political organization their political organization because it is founded on a practice coeval with their history.

Lastly, Semitic thought is a strong leaven which everywhere pervades the minds of nations, aliens though they be, who have once admitted it; and it will not easily be cast out. We have seen in Europe, even in England, a land never brought physically into contact with Arabia, how long Arabian thought, filtered as it was through France and Spain to our shores, has dominated our ideas. Chivalry, a notion purely Bedouin, is hardly yet extinct among us. Romance, the offspring of pre-Islamic Arabia, is still a common motive of our action, and our poets express it still, to the neglect of classic models, in the rhymed verse of Yemen. The mass of our people still pray to the God of Abraham, and turn eastwards towards that land which is Arabia's half-sister, the Holy Land of the Jews.

If then we, who are mere aliens, find it impossible to escape this subtle influence, what must it be for those races wholly or half Arabian who have for centuries been impregnated with Islam, the quintessence of Arabian thought? Who shall fix the term of its power, and say that it cannot renew itself and live? "Send forth", says a famous English writer, who was also a famous English statesman, "a great thought, as you have done before, from Mount Sinai, from the villages of Galilee, from the deserts of Arabia, and you may again remodel all men's institutions, change their principles of action, and breathe a new spirit into the scope of their existence."

But I must not lose myself in generalities or forget that it is for practical Englishmen that I am writing. To be precise, I see two ways in which it is probable that Islam will attempt to renew her spiritual life, and two distinct lines of thought which according to external circumstances she may be expected to follow—the first a violent and hardly a permanent one, the second the true solution of her destiny.

Among the popular beliefs of Islam—and it is one common to every sect, Shiite and Abadite, as well as Sunite—is this one, that in the latter days of the world, when the power of God's worshippers shall have grown weak and their faith corrupted, a leader shall arise who shall restore the fortunes of the true believers. He shall begin by purging the earth of injustice, fighting against oppressors wherever he shall find them, Mohammedan as well as Infidel, and he shall teach the people a perfect law which they shall have forgotten, and he shall reign over Islam in place of their Khalifeh, being called the Mohdy, or guide. To this some add that he will arise of a sudden in some distant corner of the earth, and that he will march towards Mecca, and that everywhere the blood of Moslems shall be shed like water, and that he shall enter Mecca when the streets shall run with blood. In support of this coming of the Mohdy many traditions exist which are held to be authentic by the Ulema. Thus it is related on the authority of Abdallah ibn Messaoud that he heard the Prophet say, "When there shall remain but one day of the days of the earth, God shall prolong that day, and shall send forth from my house a man bearing my name and the name of my father (Mohammed ibn Abdallah), and he shall purify the earth from injustice and fill it with that which is right." The same was heard also by Ali Ibn Abu Taleb, the Prophet's son-in-law, and by Hadhifat Ibn el Yaman, who relates that this prophecy was delivered by Mohammed one Friday at the Khotbah, or sermon, in Medina. Salman el Faris, another witness, declares that he afterwards approached the Prophet and stood before him and asked him, "From which of thy descendants, O Apostle of God, shall the Mohdy be?" And the Prophet answered, stretching his hand towards his grandson Huseyn, "From this child shall he come."

Besides this general belief, which, though not a positive dogma of their faith, is common to all Mussulmans, the Shiites, always prone to exaggerate and embellish, maintain that the Mohdy's duty is not limited to teaching, guiding, and purifying the law, but also that he shall revenge the blood unjustly shed of the Imams; and they cite in support of this a tradition of Ali ibn Abu Taleb, who thus addressed his son, Huseyn, the same who was afterwards martyred at Kerbela, "I swear to thee, O my son," he said, "I swear by my soul, and by my offspring, and by Kerbela, and by its temple, that the day shall come in which our beards shall be dyed with blood. And I swear that afterwards God shall raise up a man, the Mohdy, who shall stand in our place, the lord of mankind. He it is who shall avenge us, nay, he shall avenge thy blood also, O Huseyn. Therefore have patience. For the blood of one man he shall shed the blood of a thousand; and he will not spare them who have helped our enemies."

The Shiites say also that this Mohdy will be no new personage, but that he lives already in the flesh, being no other than the twelfth and last of their recognized Imams, who was born in the year 260 of the Hejira, and whose name was Mohammed ibn El Hassan, Abul Kassem, El Mohdy, Lord of the Command and Lord of Time; and who, while yet a child, disappeared from the world, retaining nevertheless his authority. This Mohdy they expect *when the Turkish rule is in decay*. After accomplishing his vengeance and re-establishing justice he shall rule for an undetermined period, when Jesus the Son of Mary also shall come, and the Apostle Mohammed, an apparition which will announce the end of the world.[16]

It would seem, therefore, exceedingly probable that out of the religious ferment which we now see agitating Africa some enthusiast will arise who will announce himself as this Mohdy, and head an active movement of reform. Already, indeed, two such personages have made their appearance, one in Tripoli, of whom I heard much talk a year ago, and who is now said to be marching to join the defenders of Keruan; and a second quite recently in Soudan. It is not difficult to imagine the kind of reformation such an inspired Guide would preach. Indeed his role is marked out for him in the prophecies just quoted. He would purge the earth of injustice with the sword, and, breaking with all authority but that of the Koran he would seek to renew a kingdom of heaven on the model of Islam militant. It would be a repetition, but on a grander scale, of the Wahhabite movement of the eighteenth century, and, having a wider base of operations in the vast fanatical masses of North Africa, might achieve far more important results.

Even without pretending to the rank of an inspired guide, it is certain that a man of zeal and character might in the present crisis easily persuade the Malekite Arabs to reform their moral practice, if necessary to asceticism, by proving to them that they would thus regain their ascendancy in arms. On this basis a reformation would be easy; but it would be analogous to that of the Hussites and Anabaptists in Europe, rather than of the true Church reformation which succeeded these, and would hardly be universal or permanent.

I once heard a most distinguished Alem describe the qualifications of one who should preach a reform of this kind:—"The man", said he, "who would persuade us to reform must come, in the first place, of a well-recognized family. He must be either a prince, or a Sherif, or an hereditary saint. This would secure him from a first personal attack on the ground of seeming impiety. He must secondly be an Arab, gifted with the pure language of the Koran, for the Arabian Ulema would not listen to a barbarian; and he must possess commanding eloquence. A reformer must before all else be a preacher. Thirdly, he must be profoundly learned, that is to say, versed in all the subtleties of the law and in all that has been written in commentary on the Koran; and he must have a ready wit, so that in argument he may be able constantly to oppose authority with authority, quotation with quotation. Granted these three qualifications and courage and God's blessing, he may lead us where he will."

The chief obstacles, however, to a reformation of this sort would not be in the beginning, nor would they be wholly moral ones. The full programme of the Mohdy needs that he should conquer Mecca; and the land road thither of an African reformer lies blocked by Egypt and the Suez Canal. So that, unless he should succeed in crossing the Red Sea through Abyssinia (an invasion which, by the way, would fulfil another ancient prophecy, which states that the "Companions of the Elephant", the Abyssinians, shall one day conquer Hejaz), he could not carry out his mission. Nor, except as an ally against the Turk, would a fanatical reformer now find much sympathy in Arabia proper. The Peninsular Arabs have had their Puritan reformation already, and a strong reaction has set in amongst them in favour of liberal thought. They are in favour still of reform, but it is of another kind from that preached by Abd el Wahhab; and it is doubtful whether a new militant Islam would find many adherents amongst them.

The only strong advocate of such views at the present day among true Arabs in Arabia is the aged Sherif, Abd el Mutalleb, the Sultan's nominee, who indeed has spared no pains, since he was installed at Mecca, to fan the zeal of the North Africans. A Wahhabi in his youth, he is still a fierce Puritan; and it is possible that, should he live long enough (he is said to be ninety years old), he may be able to produce a corresponding zeal in Arabia. But at present the mass of the Arabs in Hejaz, no less than in Nejd and Yemen, are occupied with more humane ideas. Abd el Mutalleb's chief supporters in Mecca are not his own countrymen, but the Indian colony, descendants many of them of the Sepoy refugees who fled thither in 1857, and who have the reputation of being the most fanatical of all its residents. The true Arabs are in revolt against his authority.

Again, it is improbable that any enunciation of Puritan reform would find support among the northern races of Asia, which are uniformly sunk in gross sensuality and superstition; while Constantinople may be trusted to oppose all reform whatever. Wahhabism, when it overspread Southern Asia, never gained a foothold further north than Syria, and broke itself to pieces at last against the corrupt orthodoxy of Constantinople. And so too it would happen now. Abd el Hamid, in spite of his zeal for Islam, would see in the preaching of a moral reform only a new heresy; and, as we have seen, the Mohdy's mission is against all evil rule, the Sultan's and Caliph's not excepted. So that, unless Abd el Hamid places himself openly at the head of the warlike movement in Africa and so forestalls a rival, he is not likely long to give it his loyal support. Already there are symptoms of his regarding events in Tunis with suspicion, and on the first announcement of an inspired reformer he would, I believe, not hesitate to pronounce against him. I understand the Turkish military reinforcements at Tripoli quite as much in the light of a precaution against Arab reform as against infidel France.

Puritanism, then, on a militant basis, even if preached by the Mohdy himself, could hardly be either general or lasting, and its best result would probably be, that after a transient burst of energy, which would rouse the thought of Islam and renew her spiritual life, a humaner spirit, as in Arabia would take its place, and lead to a more lasting, because a more rational, reform.

But it was not to such a Puritan reformation that I was pointing when I expressed my conviction that Islam would in the end work out her salvation, nor do I hold it necessary that she should find any such *deus ex machina* as an inspired guide to point her out her road. Her reformation is indeed already begun, and may be gradually carried to its full results, by no violent means, and in a progressive, not a reactionary spirit. This only can be the true one, for it is a law of nations and of faiths, no less than of individuals, that they cannot really return upon their years, and that all beneficial changes for them must be to new conditions of life, not to old ones—to greater knowledge, not to less—to freedom of thought, not to its enslavement. Nor is there anything in the true principles of Islam to make such progress an unnatural solution of her destiny.

Mohammedanism in its institution, and for many centuries after its birth, was eminently a rationalistic creed; and it was through reason as well as faith that it first achieved its spiritual triumphs. If we examine its bases its early history, we must indeed admit this. The Koran, which we are accustomed to speak of as the written code of Mohammedan law, is in reality no legal text-book by which Mussulmans live. At best it enunciates clearly certain religious truths, the unity of God, the doctrine of rewards and punishments in a future life, and the revelation of God's claims on man. Psalms, many of them sublime, occupy the greater number of its chapters; promises of bliss to believers and destruction to unbelievers come next; then the traditional history of revelation as it was current among the Semitic race; and only in the later chapters, and then obscurely, anything which can properly be classed as law. Yet law is the essence of Islam, and was so from its earliest foundation as a social and religious polity; and it is evident that to it, and not to the Koran's dogmatic theology, Islam owed its great and long career of triumph in the world.

Now this law was not, like the Koran, brought down full-fledged from heaven. At first it was little more than a confirmation of the common custom of Arabia, supplemented indeed and corrected by revelation, but based upon existing rules of right and wrong. When, however, Islam emerged from Arabia in the first decade of her existence, and embracing a foreign civilization found herself face to face with new conditions of life, mere custom ceased to be a sufficient guide; and, the voice of direct revelation having ceased, the faithful were thrown upon their reason to direct them how they were to act. Revelation continued, nevertheless, to be the groundwork of their reasoning, and the teaching of their great leader the justification of each new development of law as the cases requiring it arose. The Koran was cited wherever it was possible to find a citation, and where these failed tradition was called in. The companions of the Prophet were in the first instance consulted, and their recollections of his sayings and doings quoted freely; while afterwards, when these too were gone, the companions of the companions took their place, and became in their turn cited.

Thus by a subtle process of comparison and reasoning, worked out through many generations, the Mohammedan law as we see it was gradually built up, until in the third century of Islam it was embodied by order of the Caliph into a written code. The Fakh ed Din and the Fakh esh Sheriat of Abu Hanifeh, the doctor intrusted with this duty, was a first attempt to put into reasoned form the floating tradition of the faithful, and to make a digest of existing legal practice. He and his contemporaries examined into and put in order the accumulated wealth of authority on which the law rested, and, taking this and rejecting that saying of the Fathers of Islam, founded on them a school of teaching which has ever since been the basis of Mohammedan jurisprudence.

Abu Hanifeh's code, however, does not appear to have been intended, at the time it was drawn up, to be the absolute and final expression of all lawful practice for the faithful. It included a vast amount of tradition of which either no use was made by its compiler, or which stood in such contradiction with itself that a contrary interpretation of it to his could with equal logic be deduced. Abu Hanifeh quoted and argued rather than determined; and as long as the Arabian mind continued to be supreme in Islam the process of reasoning development continued.

The Hanefite code was supplemented by later doctors, Malek, Esh Shafy, and Ibn Hanbal, and even by others whose teaching has been since repudiated, all in the avowed intention of suiting the law still further to the progressive needs of the faithful, and all following the received process of selecting and interpreting and reasoning from tradition. These codes were, for the then existing conditions of life, admirable; and even now, wherever those conditions have remained unaltered, are amply sufficient for the purposes of good government and the regulation of social conduct. They would, nevertheless, have been but halting places in the march of Mohammedan legislation, had the destinies of Islam remained permanently in the hands of its first founders.

Unfortunately, about the eleventh century of our era, a new and unfortunate influence began to make itself felt in the counsels of the Arabian Ulema, which little by little gaining ground, succeeded at last in stopping the flow of intellectual progress at the fountain head. The Tartar, who then first makes his appearance in Mohammedan politics, though strong in arms, was slow to understand. He had no habit of thought, and, having embraced Islam, he saw no necessity for further argument concerning it. The language of the Koran and the traditions was a science sealed to him; and the reasoning intelligence of the Arab whose dominion he had invaded was a constant reproof to him. He dared not venture his barbarian dignity in the war of wit which occupied the schools; and so fortified his unintelligence behind a rampart of dogmatic faith. Impotent to develop law himself, he clutched blindly at that which he found written to his hand. The code of Abu Hanifeh seemed to him a perfect thing, and he made it the resting place of his legal reason. Then, as he gradually possessed himself of all authority, he declared further learning profane, and virtually closed the schools. His military triumphs in the sixteenth century sealed the intellectual fate of Islam, and from that day to our own no light of discussion has illumined Moslem thought, in any of the old centres of her intelligence. Reason, the eye of her faith in early times, has been fast shut—by many, it has been argued, blind.

It is only in the present generation, and in the face of those dangers and misfortunes to which Islam finds herself exposed, that recourse has once more been had to intellectual methods; and it is precisely in those regions of Islam where Arab thought is strongest that we now find the surest symptoms of returning mental life. Modern Arabia, wherever she has come in contact with what we call the civilization of the world, has shown herself ready and able to look it in the face; and she is now setting herself seriously to solve the problem of her own position and that of her creed towards it.

In North Africa, indeed, civilization for the moment presents itself to her only as an enemy; but where her intelligence has remained unclouded by the sense of political wrong she has proved herself capable, not only of understanding the better thought of Europe, but of sympathizing with it as akin to her own. Thus at Cairo, now that the influence of Constantinople has been partially removed, we find the Arabian Ulema rapidly assimilating to their own the higher principles of our

European thought, and engrafting on their lax moral practice some of the better features of our morality. It is at no sacrifice of imagined dignity, as with the Turks, that Egypt is seeking a legal means for universal religious toleration, or from any pressure but that of their own intelligence that her chief people are beginning to reform their domestic life, and even, in some instances, to adopt the practice of monogamy. The truth would seem to be that the same process is being effected to-day in their minds as was formerly the case with their ancestors. In the eighth century, the Arabs, brought into contact with Greek philosophy, assimilated it by a natural process of their reasoning into the body of their own beliefs; and now in the nineteenth they are assimilating a foreign morality into their own system of morals.

Not only in Egypt,—in Oman and Peninsular Arabia, generally there is a real feeling of cordiality between the Mohammedan and his Christian "guest". The abolition of slavery in Zanzibar was a concession to European opinion at least as much as to European force; and a moral sympathy is acknowledged between a Moslem and a Christian State which has its base in a common sense of right and justice. I have good reason to believe that, were the people of Yemen to effect their deliverance from Constantinople, the same humane feeling would be found to exist among them; and I know that it exists in Nejd; while even in Hejaz, which is commonly looked upon as the hot-bed of religious intolerance, I found all that was truly Arabian in the population as truly liberal. Under the late Grand Sherif, Abd el Hamid's reputed victim, these ideas were rapidly gaining ground; and had it not been for his untimely end, I have high authority for stating that the Mohammedan Holy Land would now be open to European intercourse, and slavery, or at least the slave trade, be there abolished.

There is, therefore, some reason to hope that, were Arabian thought once more supreme in Islam, its tendency would be in the direction of a wider and more liberal reading of the law, and that in time a true reconciliation might be effected with Christendom, perhaps with Christianity. The great difficulty which, as things now stand, besets reform is this: the Sheriat, or written code of law, still stands in orthodox Islam as an *unimpeachable* authority. The law in itself is an excellent law, and as such commends itself to the loyalty of honest and God-fearing men; but on certain points it is irreconcilable with the modern needs of Islam, and it cannot legally be altered.

When it was framed it was not suspected that Mohammedans would ever be subjects of a Christian power, or that the Mohammedan State would ever need to accommodate itself to Christian demands in its internal policy. It contemplated, too, mainly a state of war, and it accepted slavery and concubinage as war's natural concomitants. It did not understand that some day Islam would have to live at peace with its neighbours, if it would live at all, or that the general moral sense of the world would be brought to bear upon it with such force that the higher instincts of Moslems themselves should feel the necessity of restricting its old and rather barbarous licence as to marriage and divorce. Yet these things have come to pass, or are rapidly coming; and the best thinkers in Islam now admit that changes in the direction indicated must sooner or later be made. Only they insist that these should be legally effected, not forced on them by an overriding of the law.

What they want is *a legal authority to change*. Now, no such authority exists, either in the Ottoman Sultan, or in the Sherif, or in any Sheykh el Islam, Mufti, or body of Ulema in the world. None of these dare seriously meddle with the law. There is not even one universally recognized tribunal to which all Moslems may refer their doubts about the law's proper reading, and have their disputes resolved. A fetwa, or opinion, is all that can be given, and it applies only to the land where it is issued. The fetwa of this great Alem in one Moslem state may be reversed by the fetwa of another in that. The Sheykh el Islam at Constantinople may be appealed against to the Mufti at Mecca or Cairo, or these again, it may be, to Bokhara. None absolutely overrides the rest. Thus while I was at Jeddah there came a deputation of Mussulmans from Bengal, being on their way to Mecca to ask a fetwa on the disputed point whether believers were permitted or not to use European dress. A previous fetwa had been asked at Constantinople, but the deputation was dissatisfied, alleging that the Sheykh el Islam there could not be trusted and that they preferred the Meccan Mufti. Thus legal-minded Moslems who would see their way to improvement are constantly faced with a legal bar, the want of authority. *As things stand* there is no remedy for this.

An opinion, however, seems now to be gaining ground among the learned, that a legal issue may one day be found in the restoration to the Caliphate of what is called by them the *Saut el Hai*, the living voice of Islam, which in its first period, and indeed till the destruction of the Abbaside dynasty by Holagu, belonged to the successors of the Prophet. It is certain that in the first four reigns of Abu Bekr, Omar, Othman, and Ali, such a living power to legislate was accorded to the Caliphs; and that on their own authority they modified at will the yet unwritten law.

Thus it is related of Abu Bekr that in one instance he set aside a law called the Mota, though based directly on some sentences of the Koran, declaring it not conformable to the better tradition; and that Ali again reversed this ruling, which has, nevertheless, been adhered to by the Sunites. Later, too, the Ommiad and Abbaside Caliphs exercised this right of legislation by deputy; it was in their names that the Mujtaheddin, Abu Hanifeh and the rest, framed their first codes of law; and to the last the words of their mouth were listened to, as in some measure inspired utterances, by the faithful.

It was only when the sacred office passed from the sacred and legitimate House that this feeling of reverence ceased, and the living voice of the Caliph was disregarded in Islam. The Ottoman conqueror, when he took upon him the title of Emir el Mumenin, did not venture to claim for himself the power to teach, nor would Moslems have listened to any such pretension. The House of Othman was from the first sunk in degrading vices, and was too untaught to teach. The account given us by Bertrandon de la Brocquiere in the fifteenth century of the court and habits of the "Grand Turk" is evidently no exaggeration; and it is easy to conceive by the light of it how impossible it must have been for the Arabian Ulema to connect the notion of inspiration in any way with such personages as the Sultans then were. As a fact the Saut el Hai was not claimed by Selim, nor has it ever been accorded to his descendants.

The want of some voice of authority is, nevertheless, becoming daily more generally felt by orthodox Mohammedans; and it seems to me certain that, in some shape or other, it will before long be restored to general recognition. Abd el Hamid, whose spiritual ambition I have described, has, quite recently, caused a legal statement of his Caliphal rights to be formally drawn up, and it includes this right of the *Saut el Hai;*[17] and, though it is improbable that the faithful will, at the eleventh hour of its rule, invest the House of Othman with so sublime a prerogative, it is extremely likely that, when a more legitimate holder of the title shall have been found, he will be conceded all the rights of the sacred office. Then the legal difficulty will at last be overcome. The dead hand of the law will be no longer dead, but will be inspired by a living voice and will.

Since we are imagining many things we may imagine this one too,—that our Caliph of the Koreysh, chosen by the faithful and installed at Mecca, should invite the Ulema of every land to a council at the time of the pilgrimage, and there, appointing a new Mujtahed, should propound to them certain modifications of the Sheriat, as things necessary to the welfare of Islam, and deducible from tradition. No point of doctrine need in any way be touched, only the law. The Fakh ed Din would need hardly a modification. The Fakh esh Sheriat would, in certain chapters, have to be rewritten. Who can doubt that an Omar or an Haroun, were they living at the present day, would authorize such changes, or that the faithful of their day would have accepted them as necessary and legitimate developments of Koranic teaching?

It would be an interesting study to pursue this inquiry further, and to see how it might be worked out in detail. The crying necessity of civilized Islam is a legal *modus vivendi* with Europe, and such an adaptation of its law on points where Europe insists as shall suffice to stave off conflict. It is evident that legal equality must now be accorded to Christians living under Mohammedan law, and that conformity, on the other hand, in certain points to foreign law must be allowed to Moslems living under Christian rule.

Again, slavery must, by some means, be made illegal; and a stricter interpretation of the Koranic permission be put on marriage, concubinage, and divorce. That all these changes might be logically effected by a process of reasoning from the traditions, and expanding or minimising the interpretation of the Koran, no one need doubt who remembers what fetwas have already been given on these very points by some of the Azhar Ulema. At present these decisions are unsatisfactory to the faithful at large, because those issuing them have no recognized authority to strain the law, but with authority the same decisions would meet with general approval. At least such is the impression of modern Mohammedan opinion made on me by my conversation with Mohammedans. It would be interesting to work out these points; and I hope some day to have an opportunity of doing so, but for the present I have neither the time nor the knowledge sufficient for the purpose. I must be content with having suggested the method; I cannot work out the details of a reformation.

It may, however, give an idea of the kind of material in tradition which reformers are looking for, if I quote a document which was being circulated last spring among the Ulema of the Azhar. It purports to be the text of the Prophet's first treaty with the Christians of Arabia, though I do not vouch for its authenticity, and runs as follows:—

"Covenant of God's Apostle, Mohammed, with the Christian people, their monks and their bishops."—(A.D. 625.)

"Mohammed, the Apostle of God, sent with a message of peace to all mankind, dictateth the words of this covenant that the cause of God may be a written document between him and the people of Christ.

"He who keepeth this covenant, let him be called a true Moslem worthy of the religion of God, and he who departeth from it let him be called an enemy, be he king or subject, great or small.

"To this have I pledged myself: I will fence in their lands with my horsemen, and my footmen, and my allies, throughout the world; and I will care for their safety and the safety of their temples, their churches, their oratories, and their convents, and the places of their pilgrimage, wheresoever I shall find them, whether by the land or by the sea, in the east or in the west, on the mountain or in the plain, in the desert or in the city. There will I stand behind them that no harm shall reach them, and my followers shall keep them from evil. This is my covenant with them. I will exempt them in all matters wherein the Moslems are exempt. I command also that no one of their bishops be expelled from his see, nor shall any Christian be forced from his religion, nor shall a monk be forced from his convent, nor a hermit from his cell. It is my will that none of their holy buildings be destroyed or taken from them for Mosques by my people or for their dwellings. Whosoever despiseth this command is guilty before God and despiseth the pledge of His Apostle. All monks and bishops, and the dependents of these, I declare exempt from tribute, except such as they shall of their free will bring. Nor shall Christian merchants, doing business by sea, or diving for pearls, or working in the mines for gold, or silver, or jewels, even the wealthy and the mighty, pay more than twelve drachmas of yearly tribute. This, for such Christian merchants as shall live in Arabia; but for travellers and strangers in the land, they are exempt.

Likewise such as have lands and gardens bearing fruit, and fields for corn, shall pay no more than it is in their power to bring.

"And the people to whom I have pledged my word shall not be required to fight for themselves. But the Moslems shall protect them, asking them neither for arms, nor rations, nor horses for the war, except such as each shall choose to bring. But if any shall bring money, or help the Moslems in war, it must be acknowledged them with thanks.

"And this is my command. No Moslem shall molest a follower of Christ; and if he dispute with him it shall be with good manners. And if a Christian do any man wrong it shall be a duty with Moslems to stay the avenger and make peace between them, paying the ransom if the wrong demand a ransom. And it is my wish that Christians should not be disregarded by my followers, for I have pledged my word unto them before God that they shall be as Moslems in my sight, sharing and partaking of all things with the rest. And in their marriages they shall not be troubled. No Moslem shall say to a Christian, 'Give me thy daughter', nor take her unless he be willing. And if a Christian woman become a slave to a Moslem he shall be bound by this covenant to leave her her religion, nor shall he compel her to disobey her religious chiefs. This is the command of God, and whosoever shall deny it and disobey God shall hold him for a liar.

"Moreover it shall be a duty with my followers to repair the churches of the Christians, rendering them the service not as a debt, but for God's sake and for the keeping of the covenant, made to them by the Apostle of God.

"No Christian shall be compelled to go forth in time of war as an envoy or spy against his people.

"These are the privileges which Mohammed, the Apostle of God, hath granted to the followers of Christ. In return he requested them to deal with him and with the Moslems as follows:—

"1. None of them in time of war shall give assistance, either openly or in secret, to the enemies of Islam.

"2. They shall not give asylum in their churches or in their houses to the enemies of Islam.

"3. They shall not help them with arms, or rations, or horses, or men.

"4. They shall not keep counsel with the declared enemies of Islam, nor receive them in their houses, nor deposit money with them.

"5. They shall grant to all Moslems seeking their hospitality entertainment for at least three days. But no Moslem shall require of them to make special cooking for him, and he shall eat of the common food with his host.

"6. If a Moslem seek asylum with a Christian, the Christian shall not refuse to shelter him, and shall not deliver him to his enemies.

"What Christian soever shall refuse these my requests, he shall not partake of the privileges of this covenant which I have made with the bishops, monks, and the rest, the followers of Christ. And I call God to witness with my followers and command them to keep faithful to this my precept, now and till the day of judgment.

"The above was written in the presence of the undersigned persons, dictated by the Apostle of God, and written down by Mawiyeh Ibn Abu Sofian, on Monday, at the end of the fourth month, of the fourth year, of the Hejira, in Medina, peace be upon its Lord.

(Signed) *ABU BEKR ES SADIK. OMAR IBN EL KHOTTUB. OTHMAN IBN AFFAN. ALI IBN ABU TALEB.*

And thirty-one other signatures.

"God be witness of what hath been said in this treaty. Praised be God the Lord of the Earth."

In conclusion, I would urge that while it is to Mohammedans themselves that we must look to work out their ultimate regeneration according to the rules of their own law and conscience, Christendom can still do much to influence immediate results. The day of religious hatred between Moslem and Christian as such is, I hope, nearly at an end; and though political strife is unfortunately renewing the old quarrel in North Africa, there is no danger now of its becoming on Europe's part a crusade. Christendom has pretty well abandoned her hopeless task of converting Islam, as Islam has abandoned hers of conquering Europe; and it is surely time that moral sympathy should unite the two great bodies of men who believe in and worship the same God.

England, at least, may afford now to acknowledge Mohammedanism as something not to be merely combated and destroyed, but to be accepted by her and encouraged—accepted as a fact which for good or evil will exist in the world whether she will or no—encouraged because it has in it possibilities of good which she cannot replace by any creed or philosophy of her own. She can do much to help these possibilities, for they depend for the moment on her political action. There is a good cause and a bad in Islam as elsewhere in the world, and though hitherto England's physical help has been given all to evil, it has been through ignorance of the issues at stake; and I am confident that as she learns these, she will acknowledge the wrong she has unconsciously been doing, and repair while there is yet time her error.

In my next and concluding chapter I propose to sketch a policy towards Islam worthy of England's high sense of duty, and conformable to her true interests.

NOTES

[16] A remarkable coincidence of prediction, Christian and Mohammedan, has been pointed out to me in Rohrbacher's *History of the Church*, published in 1845, where by an elaborate calculation based on the Old Testament prophecies he arrives at the conclusion that the Turkish Empire will fall in 1882, the date assigned it also by the Mohammedan prediction quoted in my last chapter—that is to say A.H. 1300.

[17] This claim has been endorsed by Abd el Mutalleb, who is issuing a *Resalat rayiyeh*, or pastoral letter, this year to the pilgrims in support of Abd el Hamid's Caliphate.

V

England's Interest in Islam

Nothing now remains for me but to point the moral which these essays were designed to draw. It will have been observed that hitherto I have avoided as much as possible all allusion to the direct political action which Christendom is exercising, and must ever more and more exercise, upon the fortunes of Islam; and in this I have been guided by two motives. I have wished, first, to give prominence to the fact that in all great movements of the human intellect the force of progression or decay should be looked for mainly from within, not from without; and, secondly, to simplify my subject so as to render it more easily intelligible to the reading public. We have reached, however, the point now when it will be necessary to take different ground, and look at Islam no longer as regards her internal economy, but as she is being affected by the world at large. We must inquire what influence the material pressure of Europe is likely to have on her in the Levant, and what in Africa and Central Asia; and, above all, we must examine closely our own position towards her, and the course which duty and interest require us to pursue in regard to the vast Mussulman population of our Indian Empire.

I take it the sentiment generally of Continental Europe— I do not speak of England—towards Mohammedanism is still much what it has always been, namely, one of social hostility and political aggression. In spite of all the changes which have affected religious thought in Catholic Europe, and of the modern doctrine of tolerance in matters of opinion, none of the nations by which Islam is immediately confronted to the north and west have really changed anything of their policy towards her, since the days when they first resolved on the recovery of "Christian lands lost to the infidel". It is true that most of them no longer put forward religious zeal as the motive of their action, or the possession of the Holy Sepulchre as its immediate object; but under the name of "civilization" their crusade is no less a continuous reality, and the direction of their efforts has not ceased to be the resumption by Europe of political control in the whole of the provinces once forming the Roman Empire. The sentiment in its origin was a just one, and, though now become for the most part selfish with the various Christian states, who see in the advantage to Christendom only an advantage to themselves, it appeals to an ancient and respectable moral sanction which is in itself no inconsiderable power. It is certain that the national conscience neither of France, nor Spain, nor Italy, nor Austria would repudiate an aggression, however unprovoked, upon any of the still independent Mussulman states of the Mediterranean, and that the only judgment passed on such an act by public opinion would be one dependent on its failure or success.

Thus in estimating the future of Islam as a political body, and in view of the disparity proved to exist at all points between modern Europe and its ancient rival in the matter of physical strength, we must be prepared to see the latter submit at no distant date to great territorial losses along the whole line of its European frontier. Few, I think, to begin from the extreme west, will be inclined to doubt that, should the French succeed in thoroughly crushing the Arab movement which they have provoked in Tunis, and which will in all probability be extended next summer to Morocco and Tripoli, the beginning of the next century will see what is left of the Barbary Coast in their possession, or in that of Spain or Italy; and the greater part of the cultivable lands fronting the Mediterranean occupied by their immigrants. What France has done or attempted to do in Algiers her two neighbours may possibly achieve with even more success in Morocco and western Tripoli, for the Spaniards and Italians are both eminently colonizing races, and the hill country of Barbary is little different in climate from their own. Tripoli, on the break up of the Ottoman Empire, will certainly tempt Italian statesmen, and Spain has already a footing on the African coast in Tetuan. It is therefore conceivable that the better lands on the seaboard will receive a flood of such agriculturists from either country as now seek their fortunes on the River Plate and elsewhere. Should such be the case, the Mohammedan population may be ousted from their possession of the soil, and driven southwards, at least for a time, and a considerable decrease of the political strength of Islam be witnessed in that quarter. I do not, however, conceive that Europe will ever obtain a sure colonial footing south of the Atlas, or that the Mussulmans of the Sahara will lose anything of their present religious character. At worst, Southern Morocco and Fezzan will always remain independent Mohammedan States, the nucleuses of religious life in Barbary, and links between the Mussulmans of Northern and Central Africa, while further east the growing influence of Egypt will make itself felt intellectually to the advantage of believers. It is, however, to Central Africa that Islam must in the future look for a centre of religious gravity westwards. There, in the conversion of the negro race of the Tropics, already so rapidly proceeding, she has good prospect of compensation for all losses on the Mediterranean coast; and, screened by the Sahara and by a climate unsuited to European life, she may retain for centuries her political as well as her religious independence. The negro races will not only be Mohammedanised; they will also be Arabised; and a community of language and of custom will thus preserve for Soudan its connection with Mecca, and so with the general life of Islam. The losses, then, to Islam in Africa will be rather apparent than real, and may even in the end prove a source of new strength.

Nor must we lose sight of the possibility of a French defeat. I believe that at no time during the past forty years has the military position of "our allies" been in a graver peril in their colony than now, or the resources of their antagonists greater. It is a weakness of the French system in Africa that it has made no attempt to assimilate the native population; and it is the strength of that population, in as far as it is Arab, that it does assimilate French thought to its own advantage. It is far from certain whether the conquest of Algiers may not some day have for its effect the renewal of Mohammedan political vitality in all the Barbary Coast.

A more absolute and immediate loss must be anticipated in Europe and Western Asia. There it is pretty certain that in a very few years Ottoman rule will have ceased, and the Turkish-speaking lands composing the Empire been absorbed by one or other of the powerful neighbours who have so long coveted their possession. Austria, in person or by deputy, may be expected by the end of the present century to have inherited the European, and Russia the Asiatic, provinces of Turkey proper, while the fate of Syria and Egypt will only have been averted, if averted it be, by the intervention of England. That a dissolution of the Empire may and will be easily accomplished I have myself little doubt. The military power of Constantinople, though still considerable for the purposes of internal control, will hardly again venture to cope single-handed with any European State, nor is it in the least probable that the Sultan will receive further Christian support from without. The fall of Kars has laid Asia Minor open to the Russian arms, and the territorial cessions of San Stefano and Berlin have laid Roumelia open to the Austrian. On the first occasion of a quarrel with the Porte a simultaneous advance from both quarters would preclude the chance of even a serious struggle, and the subjugation of the Turkish-speaking races would be effected without more difficulty.

The weakness of the Empire from a military point of view is, that it is dependent wholly on its command of the sea, a position which enables it to mass what troops it has rapidly on the points required, but which even a second-rate Mediterranean power could wrest from it. Its communication cut by a naval blockade, the Empire would almost without further action be dissolved. Whatever loyalty the Sultan may have lately achieved outside his dominions, there is not only no spirit of national resistance in Asia Minor itself, but the provinces, even the most Mussulman, would hail an invading army as a welcome deliverer from him. Left to themselves they would abandon without compunction the Sultan's cause, and the next war of an European state with Turkey will not only be her last, but it will in all likelihood hardly be fought out by her.

Nor do I conceive that the fall of the Ottoman Empire and the annexation of its Turkish provinces would be a mere political loss of so much territory to Islam. It would involve moral consequences far greater than this for the whole Mussulman world of North-Western Asia. I have the authority of the most enlightened of modern Asiatic statesmen in support of my opinion that it would be the certain deathblow of Mohammedanism as a permanent religious faith in all the lands west of the Caspian, and that even among the Tartar races of the far East, the Sunite Mussulmans of Siberia and the Khanates, and as far as the Great Wall of China, it would be a shock from which Sunism in its present shape would with difficulty recover. What has hitherto supported the religious constancy of orthodox believers in those lands, formerly Ottoman, which have become subject to Russia, has been throughout the consciousness that there was still upon the Russian border a great militant body of men of their own faith, ruled by its acknowledged spiritual head.

The centre of their religious pride has been Constantinople, where the Sultan and Caliph has sat enthroned upon the Bosphorus, commanding the two worlds of Europe and Asia, and securing to them communication with the holy places of their devotion and the living body of true believers. Their self-respect has been maintained by this feeling, and with it fidelity to their traditions. Moreover, the school of St. Sophia has been a fountain-head of religious knowledge, the university at which the Ulema of Kazan and Tiflis and Astrachan have received their spiritual education; while at all times religious personages from Constantinople have travelled among them, keeping alive the recollection of their lost allegiance. On this basis their faith has retained what it has of loyalty in spite of the political Russianising they have undergone; but with their political centre destroyed, they would be as sheep without a shepherd, scattered in little groups here and there among a growing Christian population, and shut out from the fold of their belief.

Constantinople is the assembling place of pilgrimage for all Mohammedans west of the Ural Mountains, who reach it by the Black Sea, and could never be replaced to them by any new centre further south among the Arab races, with whom they have little sympathy or direct religious connection. A Caliph at Mecca or in Egypt could do little for them, and the Turkish-speaking Sunites would have no university open to them nearer than Bokhara. In this respect they would find themselves in a far worse position than the Moors, however universally these may become subject to Europe, and their religious disintegration would be a mere question of time. I believe, therefore, that Islam must be prepared for a loss, not only of political power in Europe and in Western Asia, but also of the Mohammedan population in the Ottoman lands absorbed by Russia. It will be a strange revenge of history if the Ottoman Turks, whom Europe has for so many centuries held to be the symbolic figure of Mohammedanism, shall one day cease to be Mohammedan. Yet it is a revenge our children or our grandchildren may well live to see.

How far eastward the full results of this religious disintegration may extend, it is perhaps fanciful to speculate. The north-western provinces of Persia, which are inhabited by Mussulmans of mixed race speaking the Turkish language and largely interfused with Christian Armenians, would, I am inclined to think, follow the destiny of the West, and ultimately accept Christianity as a dominant religion. But, east of the Caspian, Sunite Islam, though severely shaken, may yet hope to survive and hold its ground for centuries.

The present policy of Russia, whatever it may be in Europe, is far from hostile to Mohammedanism in Central

Asia. As a religion it is even protected there, and it is encouraged by the Government in its missionary labours among the idolatrous tribes of the Steppes, and among the Buddhists, who are largely accepting its doctrines in the extreme East. Hitherto there has been no Christian colonization in the direction of the Khanates, nor is there any indigenous form of Christianity. Moreover, Central Asia, though connected by ties of sympathy with Constantinople, has never been politically or even religiously dependent on it. It has a university of its own in Bokhara, a seat of learning still renowned throughout Asia, and it is thither and not to St. Sophia that the Sunite Mussulmans east of the Caspian proceed for their degrees.

Mohammedanism, therefore, in Eastern Asia is not exposed to such immediate danger as in the West. Bokhara may lose its political independence, but there is no probability for many generations to come of its being Christianized as Constantinople certainly must be, and it may even on the fall of the latter become the chief centre of Sunite orthodoxy of the existing Hanefite type, remaining so perhaps long after the rest of Islam shall have abandoned Hanefism. It is obvious, however, that cut off geographically as the Khanates are from the general life of Islam, Bokhara can but vaguely represent the present religious power of Constantinople, and will be powerless to influence the general flow of Mohammedan thought. Its influence could be exerted only through India, and would be supported by no political prestige. So that it is far more likely in the future to follow than to lead opinion. Otherwise isolation is its only fate.

The future of Shiite Mohammedanism in Persia proper is a still more doubtful problem. Exposed like the rest of Central Asia to Russian conquest, the Persian monarchy cannot without a speedy and complete revolution of its internal condition fail to succumb politically. The true Irani, however, have a unique position in Mohammedan Asia which may save them from complete absorption. Unlike any Mohammedan race except the Arabian, they are distinctly national. The Turk, conqueror though he has always been, repudiates still the name of Turk, calling himself simply a Moslem, and so likewise do the less distinguished races he has subjected. But the Persian does not do this. He is before all things Irani, and to the extent that he has made for himself a Mohammedanism of his own. He boasts of a history and a literature older far than Islam, and has not consented to forget it as a thing belonging only to "the Age of Ignorance." He runs, therefore, little risk of being either Russianised or Christianised by conquest; and being of an intellectual fibre superior to that of the Russians, and, as far as the mass of the population is concerned, being physically as well gifted, it may be supposed that he will survive, if he cannot avert, his political subjugation.

There is at the present moment, I am informed, a last desperate effort making at Teheran for the re-organization of the Empire on a liberal basis of government, and though it would be folly to count much on its success, it may conceivably succeed. Mohammedanism would not there, as at Constantinople, be found a barrier to reform, for Persian Shiism is an eminently elastic creed, and on the contrary may, it is thought, be made the instrument of a social reformation; only, as I have said it would be folly to count on its success; and there are certain moral defects in Persian character which do not encourage lookers-on. Shiite Mohammedanism, however, whether Persia be absorbed or not by Russia, is of little importance in a general review of Islam's future, and may safely be dismissed as not directly relevant to the main question before us.

Admitting, then, the probability, nay, the certainty, of considerable political and territorial losses northwards, caused by the violent pressure of a hostile Europe, let us see what yet remains to Islam as her certain heritage, and how the changes foreshadowed may affect her general life. I cannot myself find any cause of despair for Mussulmans in the prospect of a curtailment of their religious area in the directions indicated, or any certain reason of exultation for their enemies in the thought that with the fall of Constantinople Islam, too, will have fallen. On the contrary, I see in the coming destruction of the Ottoman supremacy, and in the exclusion of the northern races, even at the cost of their religious support, from the counsels of the faithful, an element of hope in the future far outweighing the immediate chagrin which may be caused by loss of sovereignty or loss of population.

The Mohammedan population which the fall of Constantinople would conceivably cut off from the main body could not at most number more than some twenty millions, and when we remember that this is no more than a tithe of the whole Mussulman census, and that the proportion is a constantly decreasing one, it will be evident that there is little ground for looking at the loss as one necessarily fatal to religion. The northern races still give to Mohammedanism an appearance of physical strength; but it is an appearance only, and it is given at the cost of its intellectual vigour. The political success of the Turks has for centuries thrown Islam off its moral equilibrium, and their disappearance from its supreme counsels will give weight to races more worthy of representing religious interests. Constantinople will be replaced by Cairo or Mecca, and the Tartar by the Arab—an exchange which, intellectually considered, no lover of Islam need deplore.

One great result the fall of Constantinople certainly will have, which I believe will be a beneficial one. It will give to Mohammedanism a more distinctly religious character than it has for many centuries possessed, and by forcing believers to depend upon spiritual instead of temporal arms will restore to them, more than any political victories could do, their lost moral life. Even independently of considerations of race as between Turk and Arab, I believe that the fall of the Mussulman Empire, as a great temporal dominion, would relieve Islam of a burden of sovereignty which she is no longer able in the face of the modern world to support. She would escape the stigma of political depravity now clinging to her, and her aims would be simplified and intensified. I have already stated my opinion that it is to Arabia that Mussulmans must in the future look for a centre of their religious system, and a return of their Caliphate to Mecca will signify more than a mere political change. It is obvious that empire will be there impossible in the sense given to it at Constantinople, and that the display of armies and the mundane glory of vast palaces and crowds of slaves will be altogether out of place.

The Caliph of the future, in whatever city he may fix his abode, will be chiefly a spiritual and not a temporal king, and will be limited in the exercise of his authority by few conditions of the existing material kind. He will be spared the burden of despotic government, the odium of tax-gathering and conscription over unwilling populations, the constant struggle to maintain his authority in arms, and the constant intrigue against rival Mohammedan princes. It is probable that all these would readily acknowledge the nominal sovereignty of a Caliph who could not pretend to coerce them physically, and that the spiritual allegiance of orthodox believers everywhere would accrue to him as other Mohammedan sovereignty relaxed its hold. Thus the dream of what is called Pan-Islamism may yet be fulfilled, though in another form from that in which it is now presented to the faithful by Abd el Hamid and the Ulema of Constantinople.

That Islam in this spiritual form may achieve more notable triumphs than by arms in Eastern and Southern Asia we may well believe, and even that it may establish itself one day as the prevailing religion of the Continent. Its moral advance within recent times in the Malay Archipelago, in China, in Tartary, and in India, encourages the supposition that under alien rule Mohammedanism will be able to hold its own, and more than own, against all rivals, and that in the decay of Buddhism it, and not Christianity, will be the form under which God will eventually be worshipped in the Tropics. Its progress among the Malays under Dutch rule is certainly an astonishing phenomenon, and, taken in connection with a hardly less remarkable progress in Equatorial Africa, may well console those Mussulmans who see in the loss of their temporal dominions northwards signs of the decay of Islam. Could such a reformation as was suggested in my last chapter be indeed effected, the vigour of conversion would doubtless be redoubled, independently of any condition of political prosperity in the ancient seats of Mohammedan dominion. I do not, therefore, see in territorial losses a sign of Islam's ruin as a moral and intellectual force in the world.

It is time, however, to consider the special part destined to be played by England in the drama of the Mussulman future. England, if I understand her history rightly, stands towards Islam in a position quite apart from that of the rest of the European States. These I have described as continuing a tradition of aggression inherited from the Crusades, and from the bitter wars waged by the Latin and Greek Empires against the growing power of the Ottoman Turks. In the latter England took no part, her religious schism having already separated her from the general interests of Catholic Europe, while she had withdrawn from the former in the still honourable stage of the adventure, and consequently remained with no humiliating memories to avenge. She came, therefore, into her modern relations with Mohammedans unprejudiced against them, and able to treat their religious and political opinions in a humane and liberal spirit, seeking of them practical advantages of trade rather than conquest. Nor has the special nature of her position towards them been unappreciated by Mohammedans.

In spite of the deceptions on some points of late years, and recent vacillations of policy towards them, the still independent nations of Islam see in England something different from the rest of Christendom, something not in its nature hostile to them, or regardless of their rights and interests. They know at least that they have nothing to dread from Englishmen on the score of religious intolerance, and there is even a tendency with some of them to exaggerate the sympathy displayed towards them by supposing a community of beliefs on certain points considered by them essential. Thus the idea is common among the ignorant in many Mussulman countries that the English are *Muwahedden*, or Unitarians, in contradistinction to the rest of Christians, who are condemned as *Musherrakin*, or Polytheists; and the Turkish alliance is explained by them on this supposition, supplemented in the case of the Turks themselves with the idea that England is itself a part of Islam, and so its natural ally.[18] These are of course but ideas of the vulgar. Yet they represent a fact which is not without importance, namely, that England's is accepted by Mussulmans as a friendly not a hostile influence, and that her protection is sought without that suspicion which is attached to the friendly offices of other powers. Even in India, where Englishmen have supplanted the Mussulmans as a ruling race, the sentiment towards British rule is not, as far as I can learn, and compared with that of other sections of the Indian community, a hostile one.

The Mussulmans of Delhi and the Punjab would no doubt desire a resumption by themselves of practical authority in the country where they were till lately masters; but they are conscious that they are not strong enough now to effect this, and their feeling towards English rule is certainly less bitter than towards the Hindoos, their former subjects, now their rivals. Were they in any way specially protected in their religious interests by the Indian Government, they would, I am confident, make not only contented but actively loyal subjects.

As things stand, therefore, it would seem natural that, in the general disruption which will follow the fall of Constantinople, it is to England the various nations of Islam should look mainly for direction in their political difficulties. The place of adviser and protector, indeed, seems pointed out for her. With the disappearance of the Ottoman Sultan there will be no longer any great Mussulman sovereignty in the world, and the Mohammedan population of India, already the wealthiest and most numerous, will then assume its full importance in the counsels of believers. It will also assuredly be expected of the English Crown that it should then justify its assumption of the old Mohammedan title of the Moguls, by making itself in some sort the political head of Islam. Her Majesty will be left its most powerful sovereign, and it will be open to her advisers, if they be so minded, to exercise paramount influence on all its affairs. I do not say that they will be so minded, but they will have the power and the opportunity to a degree never yet presented to any Christian Government of directing the tone of thought of Mussulmans throughout the world, and of utilizing the greatest religious force in Asia for the purposes of humanity and progress. I am myself profoundly convinced that on England's acceptance or refusal of this mission the future of her dominion in India will mainly depend, and with it the whole solution of the problem she has set to herself of civilizing Southern Asia.

Let us now see what our actual relations with Mohammedanism are, and what is the value of its goodwill to us in Asia. And first as to India. I find in *Hunter's Gazetteer*, our latest authority, the following figures:—

Mussulman Census of India

Bengal	19,553,831
Assam	1,104,601
North-West Provinces	4,189,348
Ajmere	47,310
Oudh	1,197,724
Punjab	9,337,685
Central Provinces	233,247

Berar	154,951
Mysore	208,991
Coorg	11,304
British Burmah	99,846
Madras	1,857,857
Bombay	2,870,450
Total	40,867,145

These are large figures taken merely as they stand, but in point of fact they represent far more than is apparent. To understand them at their full value it must be remembered—First, that the Mussulman population is a largely increasing one, not only in actual numbers, but in its proportion to the other races and sects of the Peninsula, a fact which I believe the census returns of 1881, when published, will amply prove. Secondly, that its geographical distribution coincides pretty closely with that of the political life and energy of the country. The Punjab and the North-West Provinces alone contain an aggregate of thirteen million Mussulmans. Thirdly, that it is homogeneous to a degree shown by no other Indian community. Though less numerous by two-thirds than the whole Hindoo population, it is far more so than any coherent section of that population, and is thus the largest body of opinion in the Empire. Fourthly, it is also the most generally enlightened. It is the only section of the community which knows its own history and preserves the tradition of its lost political importance; and if it has held itself aloof hitherto from competition with other races for the public service, it has been through pride rather than inability. What Mussulmans there are who have entered the service of Government have been men of distinguished capacity. And lastly, it is no isolated body, but remains in close communication with the mass of its fellow-believers throughout the world. The Mohammedan population of India is, therefore, an exceptional as well as a large one.

Our second interest in Mohammedanism lies in Egypt. Here, standing at the threshold of our commerce with the East, we find another large community almost wholly Mussulman, for whose well-being we are already to a certain extent pledged, and in whose political future we perceive our own to be involved. A hostile Egypt we rightly hold to be an impossibility for our position; and religious antagonism at Cairo, even if controlled by military occupation, would be to us a constant menace. Nor must it be supposed that Egypt, like the Barbary coast, will, into whose hands soever it falls, change its religious aspect. The population of the Delta is too industrious, too sober, and content with too little, to fear competition as agriculturists with either Italians, Greeks, or Maltese; and the conditions of life under a torrid sun will always protect Egypt from becoming an European colony. The towns may, indeed, be overrun by foreigners, but the heart of the country will remain unchanged, and, like India, will refuse to remodel itself on any foreign system of civilization. Mohammedanism, therefore, will maintain itself in Egypt intact, and its good-will will remain our necessity.[19]

A third interest lies in Asiatic Turkey. This we have guaranteed by treaty against foreign invasion; and though our pledge is nominally to the Sultan, not to the people of the Empire, and though that pledge is contingent upon an impossibility, administrative reform, and is therefore not strictly binding, it is impossible to escape the admission that we have a moral obligation towards the Mussulmans of Asia Minor and Syria. How far we may be disposed or able to fulfil it remains to be seen. I do not myself anticipate any further intervention on the part of England in defence of the Turkish-speaking lands. These, from their geographical position, lie outside our effective military control, and, dishonourable as a retreat from our engagements will be to us, it may be a necessity.

It is difficult to understand how an English army could effectively protect either Asia Minor or Mesopotamia from Russian invasion. The occupation of Kars has given Russia the command of the Tigris and Euphrates, and with them of Armenia, Kurdistan and Irak, so that our protection could hardly be extended beyond the sea-coast of Asia Minor and the Persian Gulf. No such inability, however, applies to Syria. There, if we *will*, we certainly *can* carry out our engagements. A mere strip of seaboard, backed by the desert, and attackable only from the north on a narrow frontier of some hundred miles, Syria is easily defensible by a nation holding the sea. It is probable that a railway run from the Gulf of Scanderun to the Euphrates, and supported by a single important fortress, would be sufficient to effect its military security at least for many years; and Syria might thus have given to it a chance of self-government, and some compensation for misfortunes in which we have had no inconsiderable share. But this is an interest of honour rather than of political necessity to England; and he must possess a sanguine mind who, in the present temper of Englishmen, would count greatly on such motives as likely to determine the action of their Government. If, however, it should be otherwise, it is evident that the success of such a protectorate would depend principally upon the Mohammedan element in Syria, which so greatly preponderates over any other.

A fourth interest, also a moral one, but connected with an accepted fact of English policy, is the attempted abolition of the African slave trade. Now, though it is unquestionable that Mohammedanism permits, and has hitherto encouraged, slavery as a natural condition of human society, it is no less true that without the co-operation of the various Mussulman princes of the African and Arabian coasts its abolition cannot be effected. Short of the occupation by European garrisons of all the villages of the Red Sea, and from Gardafui southwards to Mozambique, or, on the other hand, of the subjection of all independent Moslem communities in Arabia and elsewhere, a real end, or even a real check, cannot be put on the traffic except through the co-operation of Mussulmans themselves. The necessity has, indeed, been completely recognized in the numerous treaties and arrangements made with the Sultans of Turkey, Zanzibar, and Oman, and with the Viceroy of Egypt; and, though I am far from stating that these arrangements are wholly voluntary on the part of any of the princes, yet their good-will alone can make the prevention efficient. An excellent proof of this is to be found in the case of the Turkish Government, which, since its quarrel with the English, has given full license to the traffic in the Red Sea, which no means at the disposal of the latter can in any measure check.

At no modern period has a larger number of slaves been imported into Hejaz and Yemen than during the last eighteen months, and until friendly relations with the Porte, or whatever Mussulman authority succeeds the Porte in those provinces, are restored, slave-trading will continue. I do not myself entirely sympathize with anti-slave-trade ideas as applied to Mohammedan lands, knowing as I do how tolerable and even advantageous the social condition of the negroes is in them. But still I wish to see slavery discontinued, and I believe that a firm but friendly attitude towards Mussulmans will have completely extinguished it in another two generations. A rupture with them can only prolong and aggravate its existence.

Lastly, we may perhaps find a prospective interest for England in the probability of a Caffre conversion to Mohammedanism at no very remote period, and the extension of Islam to her borders in South Africa. It is of course premature to be alarmed at this, as it is a contingency which can hardly happen in the lifetime of any now living; but Mohammedanism is not a creed which a hundred or two hundred years will see extinguished in

Africa or Asia, and already it has passed considerably south of the Equator. Cape Colony at this day numbers some fifteen thousand Mussulmans.

It would seem, then, on all these grounds difficult for England to ally herself, in dealing with Islam, with what may be called the Crusading States of Europe. Her position is absolutely distinct from that of any of them, and her interests find no parallel among Christian nations, except perhaps the Dutch. For good as for evil, she has admitted a vast body of Mohammedans into her social community, and contracted engagements from which she can hardly recede towards others among them, so that it is impossible she should really work in active antagonism to them. As Christians, Englishmen may regret this; but as practical men, they would surely be wise to recognize the fact, and to accept the duties it entails. Nor can these be discharged by a mere policy of inaction. England should be prepared to do more than assert a general doctrine of tolerance and equality for all religions in respect of this one. Mohammedanism is not merely an opinion; a certain political organization is a condition of its existence, and a certain geographical latitude; and, moreover, it is a force which cannot remain neutral—which will be either a friend or a foe. To do nothing for Mussulmans in the next ten years will be to take cause against them. The circumstances of their case do not admit of indifference, and they are approaching a crisis in which they will, on two points at least, require vigorous political protection. Their Caliphate in some form of temporal sovereignty, though perhaps not of empire, will have to be maintained; and short of securing this to them, and their free access as pilgrims to Mecca, it will be idle to pretend to Mussulmans that we are protecting their interests, or doing any part of our sovereign duty towards them. It can hardly be argued that the Indian doctrine of religious equality will suffer from doing political justice to Mohammedans.

On the downfall, therefore, of the Ottoman Empire, whenever that event shall occur, the *role* of England in regard to Islam seems plainly marked out. The Caliphate—no longer an empire, but still an independent sovereignty—must be taken under British protection, and publicly guaranteed its political existence, undisturbed by further aggression from Europe. On the Bosphorus no such guarantee can now be reasonably given, because there it lies in a position militarily indefensible. England is a naval power, and the seat of the Caliphate must be one secured from all attack by land. It will then be for Mohammedans, and especially for the Mohammedans of India, to decide upon the new metropolis of their faith, the conditions of their choice lying within the narrow limits of their still independent lands. If Syria be still free, that metropolis may be Damascus; if Irak, Bagdad; or it may be in Egypt, or Arabia, or Central Asia.

It is manifest, however, that as far as British protection against Europe is concerned, the further it is removed from Christendom the better, and the more easily accessible by sea. I have already given it as my opinion that the move, when made will be one southwards, and ultimately to Arabia. But it may well happen that its first stage will be no further than Cairo. The Caliphate reached Constantinople through Egypt, and may return by the same road, and there are certain quite recent symptoms which seem to point in the direction of such a course being the one taken. The events of the last year in Egypt are significant. For the first time in its modern history a strong national party has arisen on the Nile, and has found full support from the Azhar Ulema, who are now the most powerful body of religious opinion in Islam. They are politically hostile to the Sultan, and though they have no design as yet of repudiating his Caliphal title, they are unlikely to be faithful to his broken fortunes, and on the downfall of Constantinople will doubtless proclaim a Caliph of their own. The family of Mohammed Ali, if popular, may then hope for their suffrages, or it may be some seyyid, or sherif, of the legitimate house of Koreysh. In any case, a Caliphate at Cairo is a possibility which we must contemplate; and one which, under the political direction and sole guarantee of England, but enjoying full sovereignty there, might be a solution of the difficulty acceptable to Mohammedans, and not unfavourable to English interests. It seems to me, however, that it would be but a make-shift arrangement, not a permanent settlement, and this from the complexity of foreign interests in Egypt, which would keep the Mohammedan pontiff there under restraints irksome to the religious sense of Mussulmans. It would be in fact but the prelude to that final return to Arabia which Arabian thought, if no other, destines for the Caliphate. The Sherif of Mecca would hardly tolerate any further subjection to an Emir el Mumenin shorn of his chief attributes of power, and unable, it might be, any longer to enforce his authority. Sooner or later the Caliphate, in some form or another, would return to its original seat, and find there its final resting-place.

Established at Mecca, our duty of protecting the head of the Mussulman religion would be comparatively a simple one. Hejaz for all military purposes is inaccessible by land for Europeans; and Mecca, were it necessary at any time to give the Caliph a garrison of Mussulman troops, is within a night's march of the coast. In Arabia no Christian rights need vindication, nor could any European power put in a claim of interference. Yemen, the only province capable of attracting European speculation, would, I know, gladly accept an English protectorate, such as has been already given with such good results to Oman; and other points of the Arabian shore might equally be declared inviolable. Arabia, in fact, might be declared the natural appanage of the Caliphate, the Stati Pontificali of the supreme head of the Mussulman religion. In its internal organization we should have no cause to interfere; nor would its protection from without involve us in any outlay.

It has already been shown how favourable an action an Arabian Caliphate may be expected to exercise on the progressive thought of Islam. That it could not be a hostile power to England is equally certain. Whether or not the Caliph reside at Mecca, the Grand Sherifate must always there exist and the pilgrimage be continued; and we may hope the latter may then be principally under English auspices. The regulation of the Haj is, indeed, an immediate necessary part of our duty and condition of our influence in the Mussulman world; and it is one we should be grossly in error to neglect. It will have been seen by the table given in the first chapter that nearly the whole pilgrimage to Arabia is now made by sea, and that the largest number of pilgrims sent there by any nation comes from British territory. With the protectorate, therefore, in the future of Egypt, and, let us hope, of Syria, England would be in the position of exercising a paramount influence on the commercial fortune of the Holy Cities.

The revenue of Hejaz derived from the Haj is computed at three millions sterling, a figure proved by the yearly excess of imports over exports in her seaports, for she produces nothing, and the patronage of half, or perhaps two-thirds, of this great revenue would make England's a position there quite unassailable. An interdiction of the Haj, or the threat of such for a single year, would act upon every purse among the Hejazi and neutralize the hostility of the most recalcitrant of resident caliphs or sherifs; while a systematic development of the pilgrimage as a Government undertaking, with the construction of a railway from Jeddah to Mecca, and the establishment of thoroughly well-ordered lines of steamers from the principal Mohammedan ports, all matters which would amply repay their cost, would every year add a new prestige to English influence. This might be still further enhanced by the very simple measure of collecting and transmitting officially the revenue of the Wakaf property, entailed on the sherifs, in India. This is said to amount to half a million sterling, and might, as in Turkey, take the form of a government subsidy. At present it is collected privately, and reaches the sherifs reduced, as I have been told, by two-thirds in the process of collection, so that the mere assumption of this perfectly legitimate duty by the Indian authorities would put a large sum into the hands of those in office at Mecca, and a proportionate degree of power into the hands of its collectors. This, indeed, would be no more than is being already done by our Government for the Shia Shrines of Kerbela and Meshed Ali, with results entirely beneficial to English popularity and influence.

With regard to the pilgrimage, I will venture to quote the opinion of one of the most distinguished and loyal Mohammedans in India, who has lately been advocating the claims of his co-religionists on the Indian Government for protection in this and other matters. Speaking of Sultan Abd el Hamid's Pan-islamic schemes, which he asserts have not as yet found much favour in India, he continues, "I may, however, add that by far the most formidable means which can be adopted for propagating such ideas, or for rousing a desire for Islamic union, would be the distribution of pamphlets to the pilgrims at Mecca. The annual Haj at Mecca draws the more religious from all parts of India, and the Hajjis on their return are treated with exceptional respect and visited by their friends and neighbours, who naturally inquire about the latest news and doctrines propounded in the Holy Cities; so that for the dissemination of their views the most effective way would be for the propagandists to bring the Hajjis under their influence. I call it *effective*, because the influence of what the Hajjis say goes to the remotest villages of the Mofussil." He then advocates as a counter-acting influence the undertaking by Government of the transport of the Haj to Jeddah, and the appointment of an agent, a native of India, to look after their interests while in the Holy Land. "By making", he concludes, "the arrangements I have suggested, the English Government will gain, not only the good-will of the whole Mohammedan population of India, but they will also inspire the Hajjis with the wholesome feeling that they owe allegiance to, and can claim protection from, an empire other than that to which the people of Arabia are subject (the Turkish).

"The proposed help would stand in very favourable contrast to the sufferings which the pilgrims undergo from maladministration at Mecca and in their journey to Medina. Moreover, practically the assistance rendered by the Government would be the most effective way of resisting such influences as the propagandists might bring to bear upon the Hajjis with a view to animate them with hostility to the British supremacy in India ... I believe if the Indian Government only wished to make some such arrangement it would pay its own way. I am absolutely certain that it would have a disproportionately beneficial effect on the political feelings of the Mohammedans towards British rule."

Such, or some such, is the line of action which England, looking merely to her own interests, may, it is hoped, pursue in the next century, and begin in this. Her Asiatic interests she must recognize to be peace and security in Mussulman India, good-will in Egypt, and the healthy growth of the humaner thought of Islam everywhere; and these she can only secure by occupying the position marked out for her by Providence of leading the Mohammedan world in its advance towards better things. The mission is a high one, and well worthy of her acceptance, and the means at her disposal are fully sufficient for its discharge. Nor will her refusal, if she refuse, be without grave and immediate danger. The Mohammedan world is roused as it has never been in its history to a sense of its political and moral dangers, and is looking round on all sides for a leader of whatsoever name or nation to espouse its cause. We can hardly doubt that the position of directing so vast a force, if abandoned by England, will be claimed by some more resolute neighbour.

The British Empire in Asia is cause of envy to the world at large, and its prosperity has many enemies, who will certainly make the distress of Islam an engine in their hands against it. Neglected by the power which they hold bound to protect their interest, the Mussulmans of India will certainly become its bitterest enemies, and though they may not immediately be able to give effect to their hostility, the day of embarrassment for us can hardly fail to come, and with it their opportunity. At best the enmity of Islam will make the dream of reconciling the Indian populations to our rule for ever an impossibility. Leaders they will look for elsewhere—in Russia, maybe, in Germany, or even France, jealous of our interests in

Egypt—not leaders such as we might have been for their good, but for our evil, and in pursuance of their own designs. The Caliphate is a weapon forged for any hand—for Russia's at Bagdad, for France's at Damascus, or for Holland's (call it one day Germany's) in our stead at Mecca. Protected by any of these nations the Caliphate might make our position intolerable in India, filling up for us the measure of Mussulman bitterness, of which we already are having a foretaste in the Pan-islamic intrigues at Constantinople.

But enough of this line of reasoning, which after all is selfish and unworthy. The main point is, that England should fulfil the trust she has accepted of developing, not destroying, the existing elements of good in Asia. She cannot destroy Islam, nor dissolve her own connection with her. Therefore, in God's name, let her take Islam by the hand and encourage her boldly in the path of virtue. This is the only worthy course, and the only wise one, wiser and worthier, I venture to assert, than a whole century of crusade.

In conclusion, I would say to Mohammedans that if I have drawn a gloomy picture of their immediate political fortunes, it is not that I despair even of these. Their day of empire in the world seems over, but their day of self-rule may well dawn again, though under changed conditions from any we now witness. I foresee for them the spiritual inheritance of Africa and Southern Asia, and as the intelligence of the races they convert shall have risen to the level of their present rulers, and Europe, weary of her work, shall have abandoned the task of Asiatic and African government, the temporal inheritance too. How long this shall be delayed we know not. Their prophet has foretold that Islam shall not outlive two thousand years before the Mohdy shall come, and the thirteen hundredth is just commencing; nor do I believe their deliverance will be so very long delayed. A "man of justice" may yet restore their fortunes; but it will hardly be by present violence or by wading to Mecca through seas of blood; and when the end of their humiliation shall have come, it may be found that his true mission has commenced already, and that the battle he was to fight has been long waging in the hearts of those who have striven to reform their ways and purify their law, rather than lament their broken power and the corrupt vanities of their temporal empire.

NOTES

[18] The Arabs believe that the Beni Ghassan, the Christian Bedouin tribe which opposed the Caliph Omar, migrated to Great Britain on the Mohammedan conquest of Syria.

[19] Since this was written astonishing evidence of political vitality has been given to Europe by Egypt, and there is now, I trust, little doubt that she will be left to work out her salvation in her own way. The phenomenon opens too large a vista to the imagination to be treated of in a note, but the Author would invite attention to it as a fact worthy of more consideration than all his arguments.